Oxford Socio-Legal Studies

MAINTENANCE
AFTER
DIVORCE

OXFORD SOCIO-LEGAL STUDIES

GENERAL EDITORS   Max Atkinson   John C. Boal
Donald R. Harris   Keith Hawkins

Oxford Socio-Legal Studies is a series of books published for the Centre for Socio-Legal Studies, Wolfson College, Oxford. The series is concerned generally with the relationship between law and society, and is designed to reflect the increasing interest of lawyers, social scientists and historians in this field.

Already Published (by Macmillan)

J. Maxwell Atkinson and Paul Drew
   ORDER IN COURT: The Organization of Verbal Interaction in Judicial Settings
Ross Cranston
   REGULATING BUSINESS: Law and Consumer Agencies
Robert Dingwall and Philip Lewis (*editors*)
   THE SOCIOLOGY OF THE PROFESSIONS: Lawyers, Doctors and Others
David P. Farrington, Keith Hawkins and Sally M. Lloyd-Bostock (*editors*)
   PSYCHOLOGY, LAW AND LEGAL PROCESSES
Sally M. Lloyd-Bostock (*editor*)
   PSYCHOLOGY IN LEGAL CONTEXTS: Applications and Limitations
Mavis Maclean and Hazel Genn
   METHODOLOGICAL ISSUES IN SOCIAL SURVEYS
Doreen J. McBarnet
   CONVICTION: Law, the State and the Construction of Justice
Alan Paterson
   THE LAW LORDS

Already Published (by Oxford University Press)

Genevra Richardson, with Anthony Ogus and Paul Burrows
   POLICING POLLUTION: A Study of Regulation and Enforcement
P. W. J. Bartrip and S. B. Burman
   THE WOUNDED SOLDIERS OF INDUSTRY Industrial Compensation Policy
   1833-1897
Donald Harris *et al*
   COMPENSATION AND SUPPORT FOR ILLNESS AND INJURY
Keith Hawkins
   ENVIRONMENT AND ENFORCEMENT Regulation and the Social Definition of
   Pollution
Robert Baldwin
   REGULATING THE AIRLINES Administrative Justice and Agency Discretion

MAINTENANCE AFTER DIVORCE

JOHN EEKELAAR
and
MAVIS MACLEAN

CLARENDON PRESS·OXFORD
1986

Oxford University Press, Walton Street, Oxford OX2 6DP
Oxford Glasgow New York Toronto
Delhi Bombay Calcutta Madras Karachi
Kuala Lumpur Singapore Hong Kong Tokyo
Nairobi Dar es Salaam Cape Town
Melbourne Auckland

and associated companies in
Beirut Berlin Ibadan Nicosia

Published in the United States
by Oxford University Press, New York

British Library Cataloguing in Publication Data
Eekelaar, John
    Maintenance after divorce.
    1. Divorce—England   2. Separate maintenance—England
    I.Title   II.Maclean, Mavis
    344.2061'66   KD769
    ISBN 0–19–825530–6
    ISBN 0–19–825529–2 Pbk

Library of Congress Cataloging in Publication Data
Eekelaar, John.
    Maintenance after divorce.
    (Oxford socio-legal studies)
    Includes index.
    1. Support (Domestic relations)—Great Britain.
2. Alimony—Great Britain.   I. Maclean, Mavis.   II. Title.   III. Series.
KD769.E35 1985   346.4201'66   85–25850
ISBN 0–19–825530–6   344.206166
ISBN 0–19–825529–2 (pbk.)

Typeset by Oxford Publishing Services
Printed in Great Britain
at the University Printing House, Oxford
by David Stanford
Printer to the University

Contents

List of Tables

Preface

In 1966 the English Law Commission made its famous pronouncement that the objectives of a good divorce law should include '(a) the support of marriages which have a chance of survival, and (b) the decent burial with the minimum of embarrassment, humiliation and bitterness of those that are indubitably dead'. The Commission's proposals for the reform of the grounds of divorce to meet these ends were implemented in England and Wales in 1971. The extent to which they were in fact achieved remains debatable. Many commentators at the time suspected that much of the humiliation and bitterness which accompanied disputes about the grounds of divorce might be transferred to disputes concerning custody of, and access to, the children and to quarrels over property and finance. We lack the evidence to judge whether or not this has happened. What is undoubtedly true is that many disputes over children and over financial matters continue to occur, and this is so within the context of a greatly enhanced divorce rate after the introduction of the reformed law. In retrospect, it seems quite clear that insufficient attention was paid, not only in England but also in other jurisdictions, to custody and financial problems at the time when the efforts of policy makers were directed at refashioning the requirements according to which the marital tie itself could be dissolved.

This book is concerned only with financial and property issues consequent to divorce. It forms part of a continuing programme of research into family law conducted at the ESRC Centre for Socio-Legal Studies in Oxford. But the immediate impulse which launched the research which it reports arose out of the growing public debate over what the principles of post-divorce financial obligations should be. This debate has followed in the wake of the change in the divorce law in all jurisdictions which undertook such reform. In England, as elsewhere, the debate was carried out in a vacuum of knowledge about what the economic lives of most people who divorced were actually like, and how they were affected by the operation of the existing law. It was primarily to reduce the extent of this ignorance that our research was undertaken. We were entering a new area of social research with what was unfortunately very limited funding. Like all researchers in this position, we may wish we could have achieved more. But we hope that what we have done will point the way for others.

Inevitably, when we came to present our findings, we became enmeshed in the policy issues which permeate this area. We have therefore used the opportunity to attempt a general review of these issues. Changes in family patterns have occurred so rapidly that society has not yet developed a consensus view of the desired outcome to the dilemmas which arise from mass divorce on the scale which we are presently experiencing. Our discussion is intended to raise questions rather than to solve them, but where we have put forward suggestions, we have attempted to indicate how they might work out in practice lest we be thought to underestimate the importance of their practical application.

As in any research of this kind, we are indebted to far more people than we can possibly list here. But we must of course first acknowledge our funding bodies: the Economic and Social Research Council, the Equal Opportunities Commission, and the Nuffield Foundation. We have received advice and encouragement from numerous individuals, of whom we should especially like to thank Jenny Levin and Stuart Anderson for their help on the legal aspects, Gabrielle Meyer for locating additional material overseas, David Piachaud, Lesley Rimmer, and Jan Pahl for their stimulating discussion of family economics, Jo Rolle for advice on supplementary benefit procedures, and Lenore Weitzman, who has shared with us the insights of her pioneering research in the United States from the very beginning of our work. Douglas Wood and his colleagues at Social and Community Planning Research gave invaluable assistance in preparing and undertaking our field work, and we are particularly indebted to Michael Wadsworth who carried out new analysis of the National Birth Cohort study at the University of Bristol and collaborated with us in writing Chapter 5 on the longer-term consequences for children of divorcing parents.

The end result, for better or for worse, of course remains our own responsibility.

JOHN EEKELAAR
MAVIS MACLEAN

November 1984

1. The Development of Post-divorce Support Obligations

I. The Legal Background

The imposition of a legal obligation upon an individual to support another reflects a societal decision about how its resources are to be distributed. But such decisions may be taken without their necessary embodiment in legal form. The history of family support obligations in England reveals the gradual translation of socio-economic organization into a legal framework. Early English law took no interest in family support obligations. 'Feudal law', wrote ten Broek, 'did not recognize the family as such or assign rights and duties to its members by virtue of membership. Property rights were the only privileges which the King's courts would enforce between father and son and husband and wife.'[1] Yet we should not assume that this reflected general social indifference to the distribution of economic resources within families. On the contrary. Whatever may be held about the true nature of the pre-industrial family in England (whether 'collectivistic' or 'individualistic'),[2] in an agrarian society families with access to land worked it with predominantly family labour. The family generated its own economic resources, and distributed them between its members. Surplus members (children) were absorbed by other domestic groups and entered their familial economic system. Children were of value to the family as a means of producing or attracting wealth and it should not readily be supposed that they were ill-used, physically or economically, by their own group. So, while early law found it necessary to develop remedies where the economic value of a man's spouse, children, or servants was wrongfully expropriated by third parties, such remedies within the family would have been superfluous.[3]

Yet there must have been casualties in this system. We can reasonably presume that these would have been taken care of, sometimes by other family groups, sometimes by religious communities. It was not until the sixteenth century that the law began to intervene in a significant manner in the economies of families by the assertion of family support duties. This happened in the context of the development of the Tudor poor law. The breakup of the traditional agrarian economy and the suppression of religious institutions began to create a drifting class of unemployed. These individuals formed a pool of labour both for the spread of manufacturing enterprise into rural areas, which began a period of proto-industrialization in England as early as the sixteenth century, and for the large estates brought about by consolidation of landholding which increased agricultural productivity. But it also left an alarming residue of unemployed.[4] In this state of affairs it could no longer be assumed that the labourer who hired out his services, or the man who left his family in search of employment, necessarily passed on his resources to other members of his family. The law therefore empowered the local poor law guardians who provided assistance to the members of a family to hold potential wage earners responsible for their support. This legislation was consolidated in the Poor Relief Act of 1601. It sought to compel performance of these family obligations by visiting penalties on 'the father and grandfather, and the mother and grandmother, and the children, of every poor, lame and impotent person', if they had 'sufficient ability' to 'relieve and maintain' such a person but failed to do so at a rate determined by the justices. This was interpreted as giving the justices power to recover the cost of the relief from the relatives.[5]

Family support obligations thus found their first legal expression in the public law provisions relating to the poor. But outside this area, the law's role was minimal. Blackstone refers to the poor law as the means by which our laws have enshrined a parent's *moral* obligation to support his children.[6] On the other hand, a husband was thought to be under a legal obligation quite apart from the poor law, to support his wife. The basis for this obligation is elusive. It has variously been seen as a concomitant of the husband's 'ownership' of his wife's labour[7] and of the legal doctrine of unity of husband and wife.[8] While the doctrine of unity was certainly seen as the foundation of a *natural* or *moral* obligation to support,[9] it was this very doctrine which prevented the development of a legal remedy to enforce it.[10] As far as the common law was concerned, the position of a wife left by her husband without support was not very different from that of a child abandoned by its father. She had no direct remedy against him. There was, however, an indirect way in which she might throw the cost of her support on her husband. The doctrine of unity subjected a wife to severe legal disabilities. She could not be bound by contract, even for the provision of the essentials of life. Such contractual incapacity could have caused significant commercial inconvenience if it had not been modified by the law of agency. While the couple lived together, the wife would be assumed to be acting as her husband's domestic agent, binding him in her transactions undertaken for the benefit of the common household. An attempt was made in 1663 to spell out a more general duty to support from this principle. Two judges of the Exchequer Chamber hearing the case of *Manby* v. *Scott*[11] sought to extend it to a situation where the wife had left the husband and he had forbidden her to make the transactions. She should not starve, they argued, simply because she had left him. But the majority of the court, as if to underline that this principle was a manifestation of the law of agency, not of spousal support, held that the wife's ability to pledge her husband's credit was strictly limited by his authority. Were it not so, control over household expenditure, which properly vested in the husband, would be lost. This insistence on patriarchal power carries with it the assumption that resources would be passed on to the wife, although the husband would dictate the conditions. If he failed to do this, it was made clear that the common law was not concerned with any maintenance claim the wife might have. This would be a matter for the ecclesiastical courts. Thus the moral rather than legal nature of the support obligation was reasserted, for the ecclesiastical courts were essentially courts of morals. Their sanction lay outside the legal system in the spiritual penalty of excommunication.

But where a husband wrongfully cast out his wife, we come closer to finding a legal support obligation. In those conditions the common law constructed an agency of necessity, binding the husband against his will in respect of his wife's transactions for essentials.[12] But even in this situation, if the husband could show that the wife had adequate means for supporting herself, he would escape liability. In 1703 the case of *Warr* v. *Huntly*[13] is reported as follows:

> The case was an ordinary working-man married a woman of like condition; and after cohabitation for some time the husband left her, and during his absence the wife worked; and this action being brought for her diet, 'twas held that the money she earned should go to keep her.

Furthermore, the agency of necessity had no application if the separation had been mutually agreed. In such a case the principle in *Manby* v. *Scott* applied and the husband's liability to third parties depended entirely on his express or implied undertaking. So if, on parting, the husband negatived that authority, he could not be sued by a tradesman even if the wife had no means. *Eastland* v. *Burchell*, which was decided as late as 1878,[14] is a typical instance. On parting, the husband agreed to make very small payments to the wife so long as the three children resided with her. The wife was to support herself from her own income. This proved inadequate and she failed to pay for meat which she had bought. The butcher sued the husband but it was held that mere insufficiency of support did not give rise to authority to pledge his credit.[15]

So as the law stood even in the nineteenth century, we cannot say that the status of marriage in itself gave the wife legal entitlement to lifelong support from her husband. If, on separation, she had independent means, she had to support herself from them. Only if his own wrongful actions precipitated her into poverty could his funds be reached, and this only through a modification of the law of agency. Nor did it matter much if children were involved. It may be wondered why, in a case like *Eastland* v. *Burchell*, where the children were as clearly in need as the wife, the husband could not be made liable for provision of food for his children. Private law, however, could not deal with the fragmentation of the family in this way. The children could have no independent rights against their father. If the wife had been entitled, on her own account, to pledge her husband's credit, then she could have included necessaries she obtained for the children as being within the scope of her entitlement.[16] But the separation being consensual, she had no such common law entitlement. Public law, on the other hand, in the context of the poor law, had strengthened and expanded family-support obligations. Legislation in the eighteenth century[17] employed the sanction of the criminal law against 'all persons who threaten to run away and leave their wives or children to the parish'. Justices were empowered to seize the chattels and enter into occupation of the land of a husband who had left his family in such circumstances, and to provide for his family from the sale of the chattels and the rents of the land.[18] In 1834 a man's legal obligation to his wife was virtually assimilated to the obligation he owed to his lineal blood relations by a provision that poor relief given to her should be treated as a loan to the husband, recoverable by the authorities against him. At the same time he was placed under an obligation to 'the children of any women he married' who became chargeable to poor relief.[19]

The contrast between the law as it affected the poor and its more general provisions is notable. The developments in the poor law reflect the continued effects of economic and social change on the family life of the working class during the eighteenth and nineteenth centuries. While it would be wrong to underestimate the extent to which, even during later industrialization, the working family depended on the exertions of all its economically marketable members for its livelihood, Anderson has drawn attention to the beginnings, at that time, of a significant change in economic relations between the family and society. Industrialization saw the growth of a pattern whereby

> one or more household members leaves the domestic arena and each is remunerated by outsiders on a basis which normally takes no account of his or her family situation. The wage received is the personal property of the individual, is dependent on the individual's own level of activity and achievement, and is paid to the individual in private, leaving him or her to negotiate with the rest of the family over how and to what extent the money is to be distributed in order to satisfy their wants.[20]

Individuals might operate from a family base, but in the work-place they were essentially characterized as individuals selling their labour in a capitalist market economy. In the urban areas, an individual's short-term economic gains in such situations might outweigh, and weaken, the normative pull of family responsibility.[21] We cannot conclude that a general breakdown of family life occurred at that time. But the perennial nineteenth-century concern with poverty and one of its perceived consequences, civil unrest, constantly saw the 'restoration' of family responsibility as a major goal of social reform.[22] The extensive legalization, and attempted enforcement, of the family support obligations of the poor formed part of the response to these fears.

How can we account for the lack of development of any such legal obligations outside that area of policy? It would be a mistake, of course, to imagine that a wife's position was uniquely determined by the common law. The ecclesiastical courts, until the removal of their matrimonial jurisdiction in 1858, assumed the power to order a husband to pay alimony to his wife if they granted a decree of divorce *a mensa et toro* in her favour, although, until the Ecclesiastical Courts Act 1813 permitted imprisonment, their only sanction lay in ecclesiastical censure. Yet when we examine the exercise of this power, we do not detect to any strong degree the assertion of a principle of perpetual family support obligation, deriving its force from the status of marriage itself. In the first place, a wife could obtain a decree only on proof of adultery, cruelty or unnatural offences by her husband. It is furthermore stated in a leading textbook of 1824[23] that:

> It is to be observed that this doctrine – of the liability of a husband to the payment of Alimony and Costs – rests on a presumption of law, that by marriage the property of the wife vests in the husband, which it does, unless

otherwise stipulated or applied: prima facie, therefore, she is possessed of no property of her own. But this presumption is continually removed by contrary facts, in which case, the general rule no longer, or partially only, can apply.

It is thus primarily the disabling and deprivatory consequences of the doctrine of marital unity which are seen to underlie the husband's liability.[24] When we look at the instances of the awards of alimony, it is very striking how much attention is given to the fact that (as was usual in these cases) the husbands had profited greatly by their acquisition of property from their wives on entering marriage.[25] The courts were doing little more than returning to the wives what had been theirs and which was lost on marriage. Frequently the wife did not recover all of it. In 1813 Sir John Nicholl proclaimed in *Smith* v. *Smith*[26] that:

> It is a rule of equity that no man shall take advantage of his own wrong. Perhaps it would be just that when the husband violates the matrimonial engagement, and the fortune was originally belonging to the wife, that he should give up the whole of it. Courts, however, have not gone to that length; yet, in such a case as the present, the court would give as large an allotment as in any.

Nor does it appear that the ecclesiastical courts found that child support raised a significant problem. They were prepared to assume that a husband against whom a decree of divorce *a mensa et toro* was granted would continue to support the children, and would take this into account when settling the amount to be paid to the wife.[27] The court could not make an independent award for the children. It must be remembered that at that time a husband's right to the custody of his legitimate children was very nearly absolute. At separation, therefore, it was very likely that the children would remain with him, or at least, that he would remain responsible for arranging their day-to-day care. It was not until the Custody of Infants Act of 1839 that the Lord Chancellor acquired the jurisdiction to award legal custody of a child to its mother, and then only if the child was under seven and until it reached that age. The Act contained no provisions about what should be done about the child's maintenance in such an event. In 1831 an ecclesiastical court was faced with a case where the spouses had separated and the mother was looking after the children. The father had promised to pay £200 per annum for their maintenance, but later refused to make payment. Sir John Nicholl observed that the court had no authority to enforce this promise directly. However, he achieved this indirectly by ordering the husband to pay the wife £1,000 per annum as permanent alimony with the proviso that if he failed to provide her with £200 'pin money', she could enforce the whole sum against him; if he did provide her with it, the total of the alimony which could be enforced would be reduced by that amount. In other words, the £200 was effectively built into the alimony award.[28]

Ecclesiastical law, therefore, as it was applied by the beginning of the nineteenth century, does not seem to have made a serious contribution to ensuring that a family's resources were properly distributed amongst its members. It was only in exceptional cases (outside the poor law) where the breakdown in what might be called the natural mechanisms of such distribution seemed sufficiently threatening to call forth legal intervention. Blackstone refers to specific laws which enforced the duty of support on Roman Catholic and Jewish parents who had cast off their children for becoming Protestants or Christians.[29] It might be thought that an increasing incidence of separation and (where available), parliamentary divorce, would have provoked concern for the economic consequences of marriage breakdown among the better-off sections of the community. Applications for divorce a *mensa et toro* in the ecclesiastical courts were increasing.[30] Applications for parliamentary divorce also accelerated during the late eighteenth century, so much so that the divorce rate was denounced by some as scandalously high. The rise was contained during the first half of the nineteenth century, but this was more a reflection of the policies adopted by various Lord Chancellors than of social change.[31] But, as we noted with respect to the ecclesiastical courts, the primary legal concern seemed to be directed towards inequities which marriage breakdown would bring about regarding property holding between the parties, or between their respective families. When judicial divorce was introduced in 1858, the jurisdiction of the courts was modelled on the practice followed in parliamentary divorce and it is notable that the courts were not initially empowered to make an order against a husband's income.[32] They could only reach his property, some of which might have originated from the wife. Yet there is evidence that, by the time judicial divorce was introduced, parliamentary divorce, while by no means available to the average member of society, was no longer the privilege of the aristocracy. Merchants, members of the clergy and professional people formed a significant proportion of the applicants.[33].

It does not seem that these legal developments were perceived as posing a serious threat to the economic ordering of that segment of the population for whom they were available. We have little evidence about how the parties, especially the women and children, to these divorces managed financially subsequent to the divorce. In the eighteenth century it is possible that many of the women whose marriages were dissolved by Parliament remarried, usually to the adulterer, but this might have become less common in the more severe moral climate of Victorian England.[34] Not only is firm sociological or historical evidence on these matters lacking, it also appears that the social careers of divorced women provided little attraction to writers of fiction. Ernest A. Baker's *Descriptive Guide to the Best Fiction*, an exhaustive review of fictional works published in England (including foreign translations), extant in 1903 refers to only five pieces whose subject matter included divorce. Daudet's *Rose et Ninette* (1892) and James's *What Maisie Knew* (1897) reveal a perception of a divorcee as an attractive, flirtatious, and somewhat unstable woman, with little sympathy for her children's (or former husband's) feelings, never short of male admirers (or the possibility of remarriage), and in no financial embarrassment. Similarly, although late Victorian 'society drama' frequently revolved around the dilemmas of women with a 'past', the concern was with the effects of conventional sexual morality on the social acceptability of those who had transgressed its codes (not necessarily by divorce) rather than the social or economic problems which divorce as such visited on its participants. Despite the increasing tempo of divorce during the first part of the twentieth century, this picture of divorcees and their lifestyles persisted well into this century.[35] But the conjunction of an explosion in the divorce rate after the Second World War and evidence from the first empirical studies has brought about a new awareness. We will return to these developments in Chapter 3.

II. Maintenance Law after the Introduction of Judicial Divorce

If we consider the common law, then, shortly after the introduction of judicial divorce in 1858, it is hard to detect in it any general principle perpetuating the duties of marriage into a support obligation after separation. Yet section 32 of the Matrimonial Causes Act 1857 gave the courts a discretion to make provision for the wife even after the obligations of marriage had been dissolved by judicial divorce, and the courts needed to find justification for creating such obligations afresh. The most difficult situation in which to do this was where the wife had been the guilty party. The ecclesiastical courts would make no provision for an adulterous wife.[36] Moderate provision for such a wife might be arranged in parliamentary divorce, although this seldom appeared in the divorce bill itself. The divorce courts started to follow this practice[37] but in 1883 the matter was still considered an open one. In that year Sir George Jessel MR observed in *Robertson* v. *Robertson*[38] that the practice had grown up of disallowing such maintenance unless a special case was shown. He pointed out that, since parliamentary divorce had in effect been confined to the wealthy 'it might well be considered right that where a wealthy man obtained a divorce from a wife who had no means of subsistence, he should, as a condition of his being granted that divorce, be compelled to make some provision for her, so that she should not be allowed to starve'. But judicial divorce was intended to apply to everyone, and 'where a working man who has married a washerwoman obtains divorce, she can very well go to washing again'. Later, policy settled in favour of permitting an order in favour of a guilty wife 'so that she may not be turned out destitute on the streets'[39] or be led into 'temptation'.[40] We observe here the importation of the policy of the poor law that a husband should support his wife to prevent her becoming a burden on the poor rate. Its application in the context of divorce was, however, curious since, while the parties were married, the power of recourse by the poor law authorities against a husband for their support of his destitute wife would not be exercised where she had committed a matrimonial offence.[41] Indeed, a *divorced* spouse was not considered a 'liable relative' for the purposes of recourse by the poor law authorities, and this is still the position. Why, then, should the divorce courts have been concerned with preventing divorced men from casting their former wives onto public assistance? But the apparent distinction between divorce law and the poor law may be illusory. Until after the Second World War, divorce was not readily available to the working classes. Family breakdown for them resulted in separation, not divorce, and in those cases the poor law liability remained. Furthermore, even if parents did divorce, their liability under the poor law towards their children, remained. Since for most of the people with whom the poor law was concerned, the fulfilment of this obligation was likely to exhaust their available resources in any case, the absence of liability to their former spouse must have been of little consequence. This is still true in an age of mass divorce.

The creation of a support obligation after divorce was not, however, entirely designed to protect the public purse. But it originally fell far short of the 'persisting obligation' subjected to so much criticism in the late twentieth century. Indeed, so far were the courts from perceiving that any support obligations survived divorce, that in the early years after the introduction of judicial divorce, they were prepared to make only the most meagre provision even for an innocent wife, on the grounds that to do more would encourage divorce.[42] When, in 1865, this policy was overturned, and reference was made to the practice of the ecclesiastical courts in support of a principle that the former wife should receive one-third of the joint incomes of the parties, the award still fell far short of keeping the wife in her former state. As Sir J. P. Wilde said in *Sidney* v. *Sidney*:[43]

> This sum will by no means place the same comforts at [the wife's] command as she enjoyed in the position from which her husband has put her forth, but it approaches, as nearly as I can calculate, the sum she would have received in the Ecclesiastical court as permanent alimony.

Scarcely more generous are the words of Lindley LJ in *Wood* v. *Wood* in 1891:[44]

> The least that a man ought to do for the maintenance and support of his wife when he so disregards his duties to his wife as to drive her from her home without any fault on her part, and practically force her to obtain a divorce, is to do what he can, consistently with his means, to maintain her in reasonable comfort, having regards her age, health and position in society.

By the end of the nineteenth century, a slightly different approach was adopted. In *Kettlewell* v. *Kettlewell*[45] the wife, who had brought nothing into the marriage, divorced her husband for his adultery and cruelty. He had an income of £19,000 and Sir Francis Jeune P. approached the question of support by asking what would be an 'adequate jointure' for the wife had she been widowed. He thought that an income of £3,000 for her would be 'handsome'.

. In 1917, however, Shearman J. enunciated a different test.[46] A registrar had made an order of £3,000 per annum in favour of the wife of a very wealthy man (who could have well afforded £30,000) apparently following a view, held by some at the time, that £3,000 was the most that should be awarded to a wife. Shearman J. rejected this restriction and said that the principle to be applied was enunciated in *Sidney* v. *Sidney*.[47] The wife was to be put in the same position as she would have been in had she remained his 'lawful wife'. Yet, as we have seen, this was not what was laid down in that case. The Lord Ordinary did, it is true, state that it would be hard to say the legislature intended that the wife should purchase her remedy (divorce) 'by a surrender to any extent of the provision to which she would otherwise have been entitled', but the remark was made in the context of rebutting the argument that a wife who chose divorce rather than judicial separation should be awarded *less* than she would have obtained from the ecclesiastical courts on a decree of divorce *mensa et toro*. Sir John Wilde thus based his assessment on the ecclesiastical principle, although he acknowledged that this 'by no means' kept her in the same position she had enjoyed during the marriage. It may have been this misreading of *Sidney* v. *Sidney*[48] that influenced Lord Merrivale P. in 1928 when, without citing precedent, he proclaimed in *N* v. *N*[49] that, in fixing maintenance, the court should take into account 'the position in which the wife was entitled to expect herself to be and would have been if her husband properly discharged his marital obligation'.

There is no evidence, however, that this 'persisting obligation' principle took a firm hold on practice. Lord Merrivale himself made no reference to it when he reviewed the situation in 1933 and stressed the discretionary nature of the requirement to do what was 'reasonable'.[50] In 1955, however, Hodson LJ approved Lord Merrivale's 1928 dictum[51] and this was applied in *Schlesinger* v. *Schlesinger*[52] where Sachs J. disapproved of the 'jointure' test. *Schlesinger* was not, however, a case of divorce but of judicial separation where the 'persisting obligation' theory would seem more appropriate. In *Davis* v. *Davis*,[53] however, Willmer LJ adopted the dictum of Lord Merrivale, noting that it had been followed in *Schlesinger*. But by far the most dramatic application of this test came in *Brett* v. *Brett*[54] where the Court of Appeal approved a substantial order against a wealthy husband after a marriage lasting only five and a half months to a professional woman of twenty-three. It was, the court thought, quite proper to take into account the fact that, had the marriage continued, the wife would have been supplied with every conceivable luxury. The court based its award on a perceived obligation on the husband, surviving the divorce, to keep his wife in this position. It is perhaps not irrelevant to observe, however, that the court had taken very strong exception to the husband's conduct, both during the marriage ('revolting sexual demands and practices') and afterwards (he refused to apply for a Get, which would have entitled the wife to remarry according to Jewish law). Nevertheless, when in the same year the Law Commission produced its report recommending how the courts' powers to make financial and property adjustment should be exercised on the introduction of the ostensibly no-fault divorce law, to be introduced in 1971, it accepted as apparently uncontroversial Lord Merrivale's dictum and adopted it as the goal to which such adjustment should be directed.[55]

Thus, when the new laws took effect in January 1971, the dictum had become enshrined in statute, although its force was mitigated by the direction that the courts were to take into account a whole range of factors and, in their light, to seek to 'place the parties in the financial position in which they would have been if the marriage had not broken down and each had properly discharged his or her financial obligations and responsibilities towards the other' only 'so far as it is practicable and, having regard to their conduct, just to do so'.[56]

During this period of development of post-divorce support law, significant steps had been taken regarding the enforcement of support obligations between people who had separated but remained married. It did not escape notice that the remedies of judicial divorce, or of judicial separation, although intended, as Sir George Jessel observed, to apply to everyone, were in fact confined to people with the means to pay for them. But the social reformers of the second half of the nineteenth century had raised to the level of public consciousness the privations of working class women who endured physical assaults at the hands of their husbands, yet who had no effective remedy if they left them; for, as we have seen, although the agency of necessity might permit such a woman to pledge her husband's credit, this would not put cash into her hands.[57] Therefore the Matrimonial Causes Act of 1878 permitted magistrates to grant a separation order to a wife whose husband had been convicted of an aggravated assault upon her, to grant her the legal custody of the children under the age of ten and to require him to pay her maintenance. In 1886[58] magistrates were empowered to order a husband to pay maintenance to a wife whom he had deserted, but now a limit of £2 a week was placed on the order. These enactments were codified in the Summary Jurisdiction (Married Women) Act 1895. No order could be made in favour of a wife who was guilty of adultery. This Act remained the basis of maintenance law as applied in the magistrates' courts until 1978.[59]

Characteristically (apart from the upper limit), these provisions gave no guidance as to how the amount of maintenance to be awarded should be assessed. In 1900, in *Cobb* v. *Cobb*,[60] magistrates had ordered a 66-year-old railway porter whose precarious earnings averaged some 23s. (£1.15) a week to pay as much as 20s. (£1) a week to his separated wife. On his failure to pay he was imprisoned, but a subscription was raised for him by 'passengers and other sympathisers'. An application was made for the sum to be reduced to a nominal amount, but the court only reduced the sum to 12*s*. (60p). On the husband's appeal, Sir F. H. Jeune P. turned to the principles of the ecclesiastical courts and substituted an order amounting to one-third of his earnings. Although this principle was disapproved of in 1930,[61] it was apparently one which was commonly argued, at least when cases came on appeal from the magistrates, so that in *Ward* v. *Ward* in 1948,[62] Lord Merriman P. rejected in the strongest sense its relevance to cases involving working-class people. The court refused, however, to replace it with any other guideline, preferring to follow the view taken in the 1930s with respect to post-divorce maintenance, which left the decision almost entirely to the discretion of the adjudicator. But the actual award which was upheld in that case seemed, on the basis of a number of calculations of the net incomes of the parties, to leave them within a range wherein it might be said that there was no significant disparity between their ultimate financial positions. Eventually, in *Kershaw* v. *Kershaw* (1964)[63] Sir Joceyn Simon P. proclaimed that maintenance should be calculated so that the wife's 'standard of living does not suffer more than is inherent in the circumstances themselves of the separation'.

The existence of the upper limit on the total sum that could be awarded by magistrates' courts, which lasted until 1968,[64] demonstrates how little was at stake in the formulation of these principles. When the income of the payer is low, there cannot be sufficient, when the household splits up, to maintain one part of it (especially if it contains the children) at the pre-existing standard of living. This was a lesson which post-divorce maintenance law would only learn when divorce was brought within the means of the mass of the population. In practice, the principle of *Kershaw* v. *Kershaw* meant that, in such cases, the economic disadvantages of separation should be equally distributed between the new family subunits. There should not be a significant disparity between them. This principle of equivalence in net result is frequently, although not universally, invoked in the current application of this area of law.[65]

But the most important features of the application of a private law support obligation in a statutory jurisdiction designed to deal with low-income earners are its difficulty of enforcement and its interrelationship with the poor (later, social security) law. As Finer and McGregor wrote:

We do not know what amounts were awarded within the statutory limits to women and children nor of the regularity of payment and the extent of arrears. But there is nothing in our examination of the history or present situation of enforcement of maintenance orders to suggest that the summary procedure could have saved many unmarried mothers or deserted wives from reliance on the poor law. Indeed, the court collecting office was not established until 1914, and women had therefore to take their own steps to enforce their orders. The poor law authorities were much better placed to arraign liable relatives and to enforce claims for reimbursement of poor relief against them. But even their success was illusory because . . . the result in no less than half the cases before 1914 was not reimbursement but the imprisonment of the liable relative.[66]

A study of support orders made in magistrates' courts in the middle of the twentieth century showed not only that amounts ordered were generally lower than the recipient's supplementary benefit entitlement, but also that 40 per cent of orders were complied with with less than 10 per cent regularity.[67] The situation had not changed by the 1980s.[68]

The position now reached repays some reflection. We have seen that, as far as the obligation between married persons is concerned, the common law intervened only where, having been put out by her husband, the wife's incapacity to hold property and make civil transactions threatened her livelihood. If she had independent means, including earnings of her own, the husband's liability lapsed. If they had parted by mutual agreement, the husband's liability (and extent of it) depended entirely on his willingness to undertake it. There was no liability at all if the wife was at fault. The wife's remedies in the ecclesiastical courts were based on very similar principles, with the additional consideration that an innocent wife should recover, to some degree, what she had put into the marriage. Nor was the husband liable to the poor law authorities if the wife had been responsible for the separation. The same was true with respect to the magistrates' courts' jurisdiction, where some attempt would be made to share the income between a man and his innocent wife, but in practice little was available to save her from poverty. On divorce, the wife eventually achieved a substantially stronger position, at least according to the letter of the law. From relatively early on, the courts seemed anxious that the husband should keep her off public funds and off the streets, despite her guilt. If she was innocent, despite uncertainty at first, she eventually achieved the apparent right to perpetual support as if the marriage had remained intact.

What can explain this progression? Without doubt the notion of punishing the guilty party and an attempt to deter people from divorce played a significant part. In *Sidney* v. *Sidney*,[69] where it was established that a woman was not to be treated less favourably because she had sought divorce rather than judicial separation, the Lord Ordinary proclaimed:

> It is the foremost duty of this Court in dispensing the remedy of divorce to uphold the institution of marriage. The possibility of freedom begets the desire to be set free, and the great evil of a marriage dissolved is, that it loosens the bonds of so many others. The powers of this Court will be turned to good account if, while meeting out justice to the parties, such order should be taken in the matter as to stay and quench this desire and repress this evil. Those for whom shame has no dread, honourable vows no tie, and violence to the weak no sense of degradation, may still be held in check by an appeal to their love of money.

Essentially similar sentiments underlie the remarks of Willmer LJ over a hundred years later in *Brett* v. *Brett*[70] when he rejected an argument on behalf of a husband that the marriage had lasted only a short time on the ground that the wife had been driven out by his conduct. There was also the view that the person whom the guilty party might remarry, probably an adulterer, should not benefit at the expense of the innocent party.[71] It is also possible, as Sir George Jessel MR pointed out in *Robertson* v. *Robertson*,[72] that divorce practice was influenced by that apparently followed in parliamentary divorce, which was mildly indulgent to the plight of the divorced wives of the better off. The result was that although the wife acquired full civil status on divorce and, since the passage of the Married Women's Property Act 1882, would not necessarily have been prejudiced by losing her financial wealth to her husband on marriage, she was treated more favourably in law than married women formerly subjected to those deprivations. The enhanced economic status of women, particularly in employment, over the course of the century further aggravated the gap between the principles developed by the divorce courts and the historical origins of the maintenance obligation. Finally, when the legislature made a definite, if not totally successful, move away from fault-based divorce in 1971, the only rationale for these principles collapsed. For if divorce is viewed as an entitlement on the establishment of irretrievable breakdown, and such breakdown is not necessarily linked to fault, there can be no basis for using financial provisions as penalties or consolations. The retention of the fiction of the marital support obligation was no longer tenable.

Notes

1. J. ten Broek (1964), 'California's Dual System of Family Law: Its Origin, Development, and Present Status', 16 *Stanford Law Rev*, 256–87.
2. See C. C. Harris (1983), *The Family and Industrial Society* (London, George Allen and Unwin), chs. 6 and 7.
3. R. W. J. Dingwall, J. M. Eekelaar, and T. Murray (1984), 'Childhood as a Social Problem: A Survey of the History of Legal Regulation', *Journal of Law and Society*, 207–82.
4. See I. Pinchbeck and M. Hewitt (1969), *Children in English Society* (London, Routledge and Kegan Paul), ch. 6.
5. See L. Neville Brown (1955), 'National Assistance and the Liability to Maintain one's Family', 18 *Modern Law Rev.* 110–19.
6. W. Blackstone, *Commentaries*, 1.16.1.
7. Blanche Crozier (1935), 'Marital Support', 15 *Boston ULR*, 28.
8. K. Gray (1977), *The Reallocation of Property on Divorce* (Abingdon, Professional Books), p. 280.
9. *Manby* v. *Scott* (1663) 1 Mod. 124, at p. 128: 'she is bone of his bone, flesh of his flesh and no man did ever hate his own flesh so far as not to preserve it.'
10. W. Blackstone, *Commentaries*, 1.15.3.
11. 1 Mod. 124; applied in *Jolly* v. *Rees* (1864) 15 CB (n.s.) 628.
12. *Mainwaring* v. *Leslie* (1826) 2 C. and P. 507.
13. (1703) 1 Salk. 118. For similar decisions, see *Liddlow* v. *Wilmot* (1817) 2 Stark. 86; *Bird* v. *Jones* (1828) 3 Man. and Ry. 121; *Dixon* v. *Hurrell* (1838) 8 C. and P. 717.
14. (1878) 3 QBD 432.
15. See also *Johnston* v. *Sumner* (1858) 3 H. and N. 261; *Biffin* v. *Bignell* (1862) 7 H. and N. 877.
16. *Bazeley* v. *Forder* (1868) LR 3 QB 559. The Chief Justice, Lord Cockburn, dissented on the ground that the mother had not been obliged to take the children with her. Any remedy on the children's behalf, he thought, should be provided by legislation.
17. 13 Geo. 2, c. 24 (1740); later, Vagrancy Act 1824, s. 3.
18. Poor Relief (Deserted Wives and Children) Act 1718.
19. Poor Relief Act 1834, ss. 56, 57.
20. M. Anderson (1979), 'The relevance of family history' in M. Anderson (ed.), *The Sociology of the Family* (Harmondsworth, Penguin Books), p. 51.
21. M. Anderson (1971), *Family Structure in Nineteenth Century Lancashire* (Cambridge, Cambridge University Press).
22. See A. P. Donajgrodzki (1977), 'Social Police and the Bureaucratic Elite: A Vision of Order in an Age of Reform', in A. P. Donajgrodzki (ed.), *Social Control in Nineteenth Century Britain* (London, Croom Helm); J. M. Eekelaar, R. W. J. Dingwall, and T. Murray (1982), 'Victims or Threats: Children in Care Proceedings', *Journal of Social Welfare Law*, 68–82; J. Donzelot (1980), *The Policing of Families* (London, Hutchinson).
23. *Poynter's Law of Marriage and Divorce*, p. 259.
24. See also *Leslie* v. *Leslie* [1911] P. 203 at p. 205: 'The origin of the wife's right to alimony was the right which the husband had to all the property of the wife' (per Evans P.).
25. For example: in *Countess of Pomfret* v. *Earl of Pomfret*, Arches, ET 1796, where the wife sought more than the customary one-third, it was said 'in reply to the observation

that the wife had brought a large fortune . . . that she had obtained rank in return and the husband had the dignity of a peerage to support'; in *Cooke* v. *Cooke*, Arches, TT 1812: 'The larger of the fortune is, the less reason is there for depriving the wife of any part of her property to support a vicious and profligate husband'; in *Otway* v. *Otway*, Arches, HT 1813, where the wife was awarded £2,000 from a joint income of £5,500, it was observed that 'the greater part of the income came from the wife'. The same seems to have been true of the rarely exercised Chancery of jurisdiction: *Watkyns* v. *Watkyns* (1704) 2 Atkyns 96.

26. (1813) 2 Phill. 235.

27. See *Otway* v. *Otway*, Arches, HT 1813, Poynter, p. 254, where the court awarded the wife less than half the husband's income because 'there are six children, who the father is bound to maintain and educate'. See also *Harris* v. *Harris* (1828) 1 Hagg. Eccl. R. 353.

28. *Mytton* v. *Mytton* (1831) 3 Hagg. Eccl. R. 657.

29. W. Blackstone, *Commentaries*, 1.16.1.

30. The number of 'divorce' cases heard in the Consistory Court of London rose from eight (1787–9) to twelve (1807–9) to sixteen (1827–9), and the number of 'matrimonial' appeals heard in the Arches Court of Canterbury rose from nine (1887–9) to eleven (1807–9) to twenty-one (1827–9): *Report of the Commissioners on the Practice and Jurisdiction of the Ecclesiastical Courts in England and Wales*, Parliamentary Papers, sess. 1831–2, vol. 24, Appendix C.

31. Stuart Anderson (1984), 'Legislative Divorce – Law for the Aristocracy?' in G. R. Rubin and David Sugarman (eds.), *Law, Economy and Society: Essays in the History of English Law 1750–1914* (Abingdon, Professional Books).

32. This was remedied by the Matrimonial Causes Act 1866.

33. See n. 31.

34. Ibid.

35. The 1932 edition of Baker's *Guide* lists fifteen works on the theme of divorce, of which more than half present an unflattering view of divorcees, especially women. A new theme, in which the plight of women is presented more sympathetically, appears in Vincent Brown's *Mayfield* (1911) and Robert Morley's *Hearts of Women* (1919), where the harshness of the law and procedures for *obtaining* a divorce are attacked.

36. Shelford (1841), *Treatise on the Law of Marriage, Divorce and Registration*, p. 592; *White* v. *White* (1859) 1 Sw. and Tr. 593.

37. See, for example, *Keats* v. *Keats* (1859) 1 Sw. and Tr. 334.

38. (1883) 8 P. and D. 94.

39. *Ashcroft* v. *Ashcroft* [1902] P. 270, at p. 273.

40. *Squires* v. *Squires* [1905] P. 4, at p. 8.

41. See *National Assistance Board* v. *Wilkinson* [1952] 2 QB 628. In *R.* v. *Flintan* 1 B. and Ad. 227 it was stated that an adulterous wife 'returns to the same state as if she were not married'.

42. *Fisher* v. *Fisher* (1861) 2 Sw. and Tr. 410.

43. (1865) 4 Sw. and Tr. 178.

44. [1891] P. 272 at p. 277.

45. [1898] P. 138.

46. *Hulton* v. *Hulton* (1917) 33 TLR 137.

47. See n. 43.

48. ibid.

49. (1928) 138 LT 693.

50. *Horniman* v. *Horniman* [1933] P. 95; see also *Chichester* v. *Chichester* [1936] P. 129.
51. *J* v. *J* [1955] P. 215.
52. [1960] P. 191.
53. [1967] P. 185.
54. [1969] 1 All ER 1007.
55. *Family Law: Report on Financial Provision in Matrimonial Proceedings* (1969), Law. Com. No. 25.
56. Matrimonial Proceedings and Property Act 1970, s.5(1); subsequently re-enacted as Matrimonial Causes Act 1973, s. 25.
57. See Morris Finer and O. R. McGregor (1974), 'The History of the Obligation to Maintain', in the *Report of the Committee on One-Parent Families*, chaired by Sir M. Finer, Cmnd. 5629, vol. 2, Appendix 5, para. 35 (London, HMSO).
58. Married Women (Maintenance in the Case of Desertion) Act 1886.
59. Domestic Proceedings and Magistrates' Courts Act 1978.
60. [1900] P. 294.
61. *Jones* v. *Jones* (1930) 142 LT 167.
62. [1948] P. 162.
63. [1964] 3 All ER 635.
64. Maintenance Orders Act 1968.
65. See the discussion below, pp. 114–5.
66. Finer and McGregor (1974), para. 70.
67. O. R. McGregor, L. Blom-Cooper, and Colin Gibson (1970), *Separated Spouses* (London, Duckworth).
68. C. Gibson (1982), 'Maintenance in the Magistrates' Courts in the 1980's', 12 *Family Law*, 138.
69. (1865) 4 Sw. and Tr. 178; and see also the remarks of Lindley LJ in *Wood* v. *Wood* [1891] P. 272, cited above.
70. [1969] 1 All ER 1007, at p. 1011.
71. See especially *March* v. *March and Palumbo* (1867) LR 1 P. D. 440.
72. (1883) 8 P. and D. 94.

2. The Development of the Child Support Obligation

I. Private Law

In the general review of the development of post-divorce support obligations in the previous chapter, we had occasion to refer to the failure of the common law to create a legal child support obligation. At most, a man's moral obligation to support his children might find legal form if his wife was entitled to pledge his credit for necessaries, for the children's needs might be considered necessaries for her. The ecclesiastical courts, too, lacked authority to make child support orders, even in favour of children over whom the father still retained legal custody, which would invariably be the case, even though they might in fact live with their mother. The Custody of Infants Act 1839, which permitted the Lord Chancellor to award legal custody of a child to a mother if it was under seven, failed to address the question of maintenance. This lack of attention to child support persisted throughout the nineteenth century. The Custody of Infants Act 1873 extended the provisions of the 1839 Act to children under sixteen, but neither this Act nor the Guardianship of Infants Act 1886 (which introduced the criteria that such matters were to be decided with regard to the welfare of the infant, the conduct of the parents, and the wishes of both the mother and the father) contained any provision for ordering maintenance payments for the child. Even the Summary Jurisdiction (Married Women) Act 1895, which allowed a married woman to live apart from her husband on proof that he was guilty of specified offences, including 'wilful neglect to provide reasonable maintenance for her or her infant children whom he is legally liable to maintain', only permitted courts (on proof of any such conditions) to order the husband to 'pay to the applicant personally, for her use, to any officer of the court or third person on her behalf, such weekly sum not exceeding £2 as the court shall, having regard to the means of the husband and the wife, consider reasonable'.[1] Nothing was said about child maintenance until the Married Women (Maintenance) Act 1920 introduced a provision that where, in such proceedings, legal custody of a child was granted to an applicant, the court could order payment of a weekly sum not exceeding 10s. (50p) 'for the maintenance of each child until such child reaches the age of sixteen years'. The sum of 10s. was taken from the current maximum payment which could then be ordered in affiliation proceedings against a father with respect to an illegitimate child. The provision was introduced as a result of pressure from magistrates who considered that £2 a week was insufficient for a woman and children to live on.[2] The Guardianship of Infants Act 1925 also permitted courts to order a father to pay a mother to whom custody had been granted a weekly or other periodical sum 'towards the maintenance of the children', which the court thought reasonable in view of the father's means, but limited the sum to £1 per child per week (the then current limit under affiliation law) when granted by a magistrates' court.[3]

The reluctance to introduce statutory machinery for enforcing the moral obligation that a parent should support his children in these situations may partly be explained by the fact that, though they are circumstances in which the parents will have separated, they remain legally married. Any remedy on behalf of the children was absorbed by the remedies, so far as they existed, available to the spouse. At least this was the view taken by the majority of the court in *Bazeley* v. *Forder*.[4] Here the parties were separated and the wife had the custody of the children aged under seven. The question was whether the father could be held liable for the provision of clothes supplied to the children at the wife's behest. In a dissenting opinion, Lord Cockburn CJ observed that when, in 1839, Parliament had permitted custody of children under seven to be awarded to a mother, it seemed to have overlooked the possibility that she might not have the means to support them. In his view, it was not open to the court to remedy this omission. The majority, however, thought that the children's expenses could be considered part of the wife's, and the father held liable accordingly. The assimilation of the children's needs to those of their caregiver therefore followed from the assimilation of the remedies and must explain the absence of separate provision for child maintenance in these late nineteenth century statutes. The power to make specific additions to the wife's maintenance related to each child for whom she was caring, introduced in 1920, was not the result of any reappraisal of the elements of the award, for example, by breaking it down into segments which were properly attributable to the wife and to the children, but simply reflected the view that the maximum global sum then permitted (£2 per week) was too low for a one-parent family.

Where, however, divorce had severed the marital tie and, accordingly, the inter-spousal maintenance obligation, a new basis had to be found for ordering maintenance, not only between spouses, but also with respect to children. Indeed, such a basis was provided in the Matrimonial Causes Act 1857, section 35 of which enacted that in any suit for judicial separation, nullity, or divorce, the court might 'make such provision in the final decree as it may deem just and proper with respect to the Custody, Maintenance and Education of the Children of the Marriage of Whose Parents is the Subject of such Suit'. We have already considered the uncertainty surrounding the criteria thought relevant for awarding support to a former spouse. About the basis for awarding child support there was even less clarity. In 1929 a leading practitioner's book observed that, with regard to maintenance after divorce, 'the amount usually allotted is that required to bring up the income of the wife to one-third of the joint incomes of the parties. In addition a further allowance may be made for the maintenance of the children of the marriage'.[5] Sometimes, no doubt, when a relatively certain figure could be put on expenditure on a child, as in the case of school fees and where the father could afford to pay them, the 'further allowance' for the children's maintenance could be put on a rational basis. On other occasions judges seemed to be making some attempt at assessing (one might almost say, guessing) what was necessary to spend on a child. In *Todd* v. *Todd* in 1873,[6] for example, where a wife received £196 a year from property settled on her by her husband and the husband's annual income was £367, Hannen P. awarded the wife an extra £90 to cover the expenses of the three children. This additional award raised the wife's total income from 35 per cent of the parties' joint income to one half of it. One hundred years later, in *Wachtel* v. *Wachtel*,[7] the trial judge had made an award (for one child) which likewise had the effect of bringing up the amount awarded on the wife's account alone from one-third to what was considered 'almost half' of the husband's gross income. Without explanation, other than asserting that it was 'much too high', the Court of Appeal cut the award for the child by nearly half (from £500 to £300 per annum), leaving the wife with some 37 per cent of the (notional) joint incomes. It is difficult to see any rationale in this process; the courts have made no attempt to give any, and none can be found in the leading texts.

Splitting maintenance for the child from the wife's award might have enabled courts to mitigate the effect on the children of the reduction of maintenance payable to the wife on the ground of her misconduct.[8] But apart from that circumstance, it is difficult to find what purpose the distinction served. It was, in fact, a source of considerable difficulty. This was especially so in the magistrates' courts. The powers of these courts to make awards were, as we have seen, subject to statutory limits. As the Committee on Statutory Maintenance Limits observed in 1968, the reasons why limits were imposed are obscure.[9] Parliament may well have simply wished to avoid conferring too wide powers on a lay tribunal. On the other hand, the first time limits were imposed was when the Poor Law Amendment Act of 1844 allowed the mother of an illegitimate child to claim maintenance directly from the father. The Committee noted the close relationship between this jurisdiction and poor law policy, which was then governed by the principle of 'less eligibility'. Only ten years earlier, in an express attempt at deterring illegitimate pregnancies, Parliament had removed from mothers the right to bring the father before magistrates to whom he might be required to give security to indemnify the parish for expenditure incurred in supporting his child. Women were to be made to bear the burden of their 'licentiousness', alone.[10] In restoring to such women the power to mobilize legal machinery to secure income to meet the consequences of their 'offence', Parliament may have felt it appropriate to put a severe restriction on the sums which could be ordered in their favour. The amounts permitted could hardly have been thought to be sufficient fully to maintain both mother and child as a family unit. The original limit was 2s. 6d. (12½p) a week. In 1960 the sum allowed was only 50s. (£2.50) a week and remained thus even at a time when the Committee considered that at least £9 a week was needed to meet the expenses of a first child.[11] Yet, as we have seen, the amounts of the additions permitted for children of separated wives were taken from those laid down for illegitimate children under the affiliation law.

Apart from the questionable derivation of the limits placed upon the additional sums permitted to be awarded for children in magistrates' courts, the Committee on Statutory Maintenance Limits recognized that:

> some of the needs of a family cannot be assessed in an individual payment. The cost of such items as rent, rates, mortgage payments and heating bills is only marginally affected by the number of members of the family. It would be impracticable to order maintenance in such a way that separate provision was made for each item of this kind. To a large extent, therefore, allocation of separate amounts to a wife and to individual children must always be arbitrary.[12]

In 1960 the maximum allocation was fixed at £7. 10s. (£7.50) for the maintenance of a spouse and 50s. (£2.50) for the maintenance of a child. But, as originally introduced in 1920, the additions for children served no purpose other than to increase the total amount which could be ordered in favour of the wife. The fact that they were designated as child maintenance meant little. As Lord Merriman explained in *Kinnane* v. *Kinnane*[13] and again *Cooke* v. *Cooke*,[14] the applicant and beneficiary of the order remained the wife. 'We talk loosely of an order for the children. It is not an order for the children . . . any sum ordered to be paid to the wife for the support of the children is, as it always has been, an order for the wife.' So, even if the husband's dereliction lay in failing to support the children, the order would be in favour of the wife. Conversely, 'however badly the husband has behaved in respect of the infant child, there may be a complete and absolute bar to the wife obtaining an order if she has committed adultery'.[15] However, if the wife was not barred from the remedy by her misconduct, but merely failed to establish that the husband was in breach of any duty to maintain her, as, for example, if they had separated consensually without his undertaking to continue to support her, then she was entitled to claim that he was not supporting the children. Since the children's claims merged with the wife's, if she proved wilful neglect to support the children, the court could make an order for the wife on her own account with the supplements for the children. This is what the magistrates had done in *Starke* v. *Starke* (*No. 2*),[16] awarding £1 per week for the wife and 30*s*. (£1.50) per week for the child, and Lord Merriman P. confirmed that they had jurisdiction to do so. However, the President complicated the issue further by saying that, since the magistrates had made the maximum award for the child, and the wife had failed to establish a claim in her own right, her award should be reduced to a nominal sum, thus bringing about a drastic reduction in the income of that single-parent household.

The Matrimonial Proceedings (Magistrates' Courts) Act 1960 formally separated the claims of wife and child. Thus it was held in *Young* v. *Young*[17] that if a husband was liable for wilful neglect to maintain the child, no order could be made in favour of the wife unless she was entitled to it in her own right. But equally, it was now possible to make an order in favour of the child even if the wife had committed a matrimonial offence.[18] Difficulty now arose as a result of the limits which were set on the maximum amounts which magistrates were allowed to order either for the wife or for each child. If the wife's claim was barred, yet neglect of the child made out, the limit meant that only a very unsatisfactory order could be made for the child. The issue came to a head in *Northrop* v. *Northrop*.[19] Here the parting was consensual, so the wife's claim was not barred by misconduct. However, she could not show that the husband had undertaken to maintain her during this separation, so he could not be guilty of wilful neglect respecting her. Sir Jocelyn Simon P., in the Divisional Court, thought that in such a case, if the husband neglected his obligations to the child, the court could also find wilful neglect of the wife. The reason was the 'close identification of the interest between mother and dependent child so that a failure to maintain the child throws the obligation on to its mother and amounts to wilful neglect to maintain her'. The Court of Appeal, however, rejected this reasoning for, as we have seen, the view was now taken that the 1960 Act separated the claim of mother and child. However, the Court of Appeal also wished to reach a result which would permit a global award to be made which exceeded the limit set down for the child maintenance. Willmer LJ did this by arguing that, where parties separated by agreement, leaving the child with the wife, an undertaking could be *implied* that the husband should support the wife. If he failed to keep it, he would be guilty of wilful neglect to maintain her. Winn and Diplock LJ found an alternative way of boosting the order. They argued that, if wilful neglect of the child was established, a court could order not only child maintenance (within the statutory limits) but also payments to the wife, within the limits set down for 'wife' maintenance, even though no finding of wilful neglect to maintain her could be made. They were careful, however, to say that this order would not necessarily be for the wife's 'maintenance' but would be a sum which was 'reasonably necessary to enable her to make proper provision for the needs of the child' (Winn LJ). In Diplock LJ's words:

> The child must be clothed, housed and tended by the wife. This then would be adequate for herself if living alone. It may also involve her in loss of earnings in so far as her inability to take paid employment is restricted by the child's need for her personal care.[20]

The importance of *Northrop* v. *Northrop* lies in its recognition of the fact that, for a large part, a child's and its caregiver's needs are coincident and its acceptance that if the award was limited to the maximum then allowed for child maintenance, that would have been insufficient to fulfil those needs. The limits on the awards which magistrates' courts could make were abolished in 1968,[21] and in the present day, juggling of the award between an element for the child and an element for the wife is unnecessary. This is well illustrated in *Haroutanian* v. *Jennings*.[22] If a child is illegitimate, the father cannot be ordered to maintain its mother in the same way a husband (or former husband) can be required to support his wife (or former wife). The only order that can be made is for the support of the child. The limits to these orders, which, as we saw, formed the basis for the limits to the orders which magistrates could make for legitimate children, were also removed in 1968. It was held, in *Haroutanian* v. *Jennings*, that in fixing the amount of the order in favour of an illegitimate child, magistrates could take into account the fact that the mother had given up work to look after the child and that the award could, accordingly, include an element for her own support. The way would seem to be open, in child cases, to assimilating the needs of the child and its caregiver, at least to a large extent, and reaching a more rational basis for calculating child maintenance. However, this has not come about. One reason has undoubtedly been the persistence of the view that a separated or divorced husband does indeed owe an obligation to his wife (or former wife) in her own right. But further causes are to be found in the structure of tax and social security law.

The basic tax principle governing maintenance payments is that the husband (assuming him to be the payer) is not liable to pay tax on maintenance paid to his wife under a court order or by agreement. The money is treated as the income of the recipient. This means that the wife (the position of the child will be considered separately) must declare what she receives for tax purposes. For convenience, however, the husband usually deducts tax at the standard rate from the gross amount he has been ordered to pay her, and hands over the remaining sum. The wife then calculates the tax for which she would have been liable if she had received the whole sum. If this turns out to be less than the amount the husband withheld, she can claim for repayment of the difference. For a wife this can be a matter of some complexity and in any case entails a delay in receiving what she is really due. In 1944, a different procedure was laid down for 'small maintenance payments'.[23] When the amount ordered falls within prescribed limits, the husband pays it in full, without deduction for tax, though of course the wife is assessed on the full amount she receives and will have to make the tax payment. The reform also made it easier for magistrates when calculating arrears due under small orders: they no longer needed to make tax deductions in ascertaining the net sum due.

In fixing the limits for 'small maintenance payments', legislation has maintained the distinction between spouse and child maintenance. Currently the limits are £33 per week (or £143 per month) for a spouse or former spouse and £18 a week (or £78 a month) for a person under twenty-one.[24] The assumption that child maintenance is lower than maintenance of the adult, is characteristic. However, provided the combined amount of the two elements does not exceed the total of the limit, it normally matters not whether the maintenance is ascribed to the adult or the child. But in some circumstances it does matter. One of the most important is where the child support is ordered to be paid *direct* to the child, rather than (as was usual) to the adult *for* the child. The advantage of doing this was first noted by *Rayden on Divorce* in the sixth edition, 1953:[25]

> A new form of order has recently been occasionally adopted in cases where it has been necessary to provide substantial sums for the education expenses of children as well as for their general maintenance. This form provides for payment to be made to the child direct. The effect is that the child becomes an ordinary taxable individual, with a single person's tax reliefs. If the child has not already an income from other sources, it follows that an order for any amount not exceeding £150 a year less tax will yield, after recovery, by rebates, of the tax deducted, the whole sum ordered.

The scope for making orders direct to the children increased when the High Court acquired power, in 1970, to make such orders in maintenance proceedings unrelated to divorce, nullity, or judicial separation proceedings[26] and, most importantly, when this power was conferred on magistrates' courts under the Domestic Proceedings and Magistrates' Courts Act 1978.[27] Divorce court orders can be registered in magistrates' courts for enforcement purposes and in 1977, a Practice Direction required all orders for maintenance payments direct to the children made by those courts, to contain a clause whereby receipt by the caregiving parent would be sufficient to discharge any payment made under the order.[28] This manoeuvre, as well as some arrangements concerning payment of school fees, illustrates the patent artificiality of the procedure.[29] For the reality remains the same as it always was, whether the maintenance is expressed as payable to the parent on the child's behalf or directly to the child: it will be the caregiving parent who will in practice invariably collect the money and manage it. This will indeed be the expectation of everyone concerned, but care must be taken that this is not made a *legal* requirement regarding the child's portion, because that would make the support payment a *settlement*, and the sum paid would no longer be deductible from the payer's income for tax purposes.[30] However, if the right formulae are used and the calculations are correctly made, the formal allocation of the total award between adult and child can, in some cases, achieve important tax savings.

Similar points once arose in connection with social security law.[31] At one time an order that maintenance should be paid direct to the child had advantages if the mother caring for the child was in receipt of supplementary benefit. This was because supplementary benefit, like maintenance, is structured in such a way that the major portion of the benefit is payable on the adult claimant's own account, but additions may be made for dependent children in his or her care. It was once argued that, where the child had independent income in excess of the additional amount allowed for the child, *the mother* was no longer bound to meet his requirements, for these were being met by that income. Since a child's income was to be aggregated with the mother's for the purposes of assessing her entitlement to supplementary benefit only if she was so bound, it followed that, in these circumstances, aggregation should not take place, thus permitting her to qualify for supplementary benefit and at the same time retain the child's income.[32] This argument was, however, rejected by the House of Lords in *Supplementary Benefits Commission* v. *Jull, Y* v. *Supplementary Benefits Commission.*[33] The caregiving mother remained bound to meet her child's requirements quite irrespective of the availability of external income for the child, which should be aggregated accordingly. The same point was made with respect to assessment of entitlement to Family Income Supplement. The income of a child was generally excluded in calculating the gross income of a family,[34] thus increasing the availability of the benefit if maintenance was ordered direct to the child. But a regulation, introduced in 1980, removed this exclusion in the case of income 'derived directly or indirectly from a parent or other person under a legal obligation to maintain him'.[35] This qualification blocked another possible method whereby specification that maintenance was payable direct to a child might have given the recipient family advantages not available if the payment was to be made to the adult with respect to the child.

It thus appears that, while the advantages of splitting the award between adult and child as far as welfare benefits are concerned have been removed, advantages may still be found under tax law. Such an inequity between the poor and the better off is clearly indefensible. But, social injustice aside, the intricacies raise serious questions about the appropriateness of the traditional method of structuring maintenance awards in cases involving families with dependent children. Of course, a family's 'needs' increase when a child is introduced into it, and grow with each additional child. It is right that the family's entitlement to benefits, or, where relevant, to maintenance, should expand accordingly. But to suppose that the increments can in any way sensibly correspond to the needs of the individual children, in isolation, is to ignore elementary principles of financing and marginal costing.

II. Public Law

In the first chapter we described the way in which family support obligations were imposed originally in the Tudor poor law, and how this system developed in the nineteenth century. The Poor Relief Act of 1834, as amended throughout the following years, formed the foundation of the legal structure of the poor law until 1948. Its abolition by the National Assistance Act 1948 saw a reformulation of the intra-familial duties. The duties of parents towards their children and of a husband towards his wife remained. But now a wife owed a similar duty to her husband,[36] and the duties of grandparents and of children towards their parents and grandparents were removed.[37] These provisions have been incorporated into the modern law governing supplementary benefit payments.[38] Their most important function is to provide a mechanism whereby the state can recoup from the liable relative some of the costs of its welfare budget. The value of this function will be considered when the whole question of the relationship between private maintenance law and public support is reviewed at the conclusion of this book. At this point we would draw attention only to a number of problems in the nature of the parental obligation, as expressed in the present law, which are analogous to the weakness in the structure of the private law remedies discussed earlier.

In *National Assistance Board* v. *Wilkinson*,[39] a wife was being supported by the Board after she had refused to join her husband in accommodation found by him. The Board applied for recovery of its expenditure from the husband, but failed both before the magistrates and the Divisional Court. The reason was that, by putting herself in desertion, the wife had forefeited her common law right to maintenance from her husband, and the Board could have no greater rights than the wife. This reasoning was later rejected by the Court of Appeal in *National Assistance Board* v. *Parkes*[40] on the ground that the statutory provisions constitute a self-contained code and are not to be read as subject to a superimposed common law doctrine. However, the court thought that the actual decision in *Wilkinson* was correct because, although under the statute a husband's obligation was not automatically abrogated by his wife's commission of a matrimonial offence, that fact was a relevant, perhaps conclusive, circumstance as to whether he should be required to pay. The point to which we wish to draw attention is that, in *Wilkinson*, the wife had custody of the child of the marriage. The husband had continued to pay her 15*s.* (75p) per week for the child and was charged only for the £1. 4*s.* 6*d.* (£1.25) per week which he had stopped paying the wife and for the provision of which the Board now sought recovery. The effect of this splitting of the liability between wife and child is that, where the husband's duty towards his wife is absolved, his duty to recompense the state with respect to his child's maintenance is confined to the 'child element' of the state's payment to the mother.

The position is clearer in the case of divorce or where the parents were never married. For in those cases, the poor law imposed, and still imposes, no duty between the adults. The state can therefore recover only those payments attributable to the child, that is, the current scale rates for children. But in fact the child will also benefit (and it is assumed he will do so) from the basic sum paid to the claimant adult. For this benefit there is no recourse against the liable relative. The result is that the extent to which the legal duty of the parent to support the child is enforced by way of the liable relative provisions is as arbitrary as the division of the benefit itself between the basic sum payable to the claimant and the additions made for the children. But the situation is even worse than that. It is relatively rare for the officials of the Department of Health and Social Security (who administer the supplementary benefit system) to take proceedings on their own initiative against liable relatives.[41] More commonly the former wife will have a court maintenance order in favour of herself and the children which will (in total) amount to a sum less than she would receive by claiming supplementary benefit in full. Since income from a former spouse is taken into account in computing a claimant's income for the purpose of assessing liability for supplementary benefit, a procedure (known as the 'diversion procedure') is widely used by which the mother assigns the whole benefit of the order in favour of the Department in return for her full supplementary benefit entitlement. If the payments fall into arrears, the clerk of the court may, with the mother's authorization, enforce it in full against the debtor. If this procedure is used, therefore, the state will recoup from the father payments he makes to his former wife on her own account as well as the child additions. But, confusingly, these payments are deductible in computing the father's income for tax purposes, whereas payments made directly by him to the Department are not.[42]

Inconsistency does not stop there. As will be seen in later chapters, divorced mothers living alone with dependent children rely in significant numbers on supplementary benefit as their major source of income. The Committee on One-Parent Families (Finer Committee) recommended the introduction of a 'guaranteeed maintenance allowance' for all one-parent families on a scale more generous than the then exisiting (and present) supplementary benefit scale rates. This has been rejected, primarily for financial reasons, but in its stead a number of fragmented measures have been taken to augment the social security provision available for one-parent families. One of these is that child benefit, which is available to all families with dependent children irrespective of means, is more generous towards these families by reason of an addition (known as One Parent Benefit) which is made to the amount of benefit payable with respect to a first child. Another is that, where a lone parent is in full-time work, (she) may be entitled to Family Income Supplement (which is universally available to families on low incomes) on terms which are more generous than those applicable to other families. She will qualify if she works for twenty-four hours a week rather than the thirty hours required of other claimants and the level below which her income must fall in order to qualify for the benefit is the same as that prescribed for two-adult families, which it is more likely to do. These two sources of public assistance can help a lone parent only if she is not drawing supplementary benefit because any income from them will be taken into account when assessing entitlement to supplementary benefit. But where, for example, the mother is in full-time work and boosts her net income from those sources, there is no machinery by which the state may have recourse against the father to recover their value. Similarly, if she is earning sufficient to qualify for taxation, a single parent is given a more generous personal allowance (the 'additional personal allowance') than other single taxpayers, but this loss to the revenue cannot be reclaimed from the liable relative. But should she work part-time, or not at all, and fall back on supplementary benefit, the state's right to 'enforce' the child support obligation against the father revives. It is notable that the Finer Committee's proposed allowance, being conceived of as a *child's* allowance (although containing a substantial element of support for the child's caregiver) would have, in principle, been recoverable in full from the liable relative.[44] Such equity of treatment of liable relatives seems impossible to achieve under the system of fragmented benefits presently in operation.

Notes

1. Summary Jurisdiction (Married Women) Act 1895, s. 4.
2. See 42 HL Deb. col. 712 (1920).
3. Guardianship of Infants Act 1925, s. 3 (2). For an account of the parliamentary history of this Act, see *Report of the Committee on Statutory Maintenance Limits* (1968), (Cmnd. 3587), Appendix B.
4. (1868) LR 3 QB 559.
5. Phillips (1929), *The Practice of the Divorce Division*, p. 188.
6. (1873) 42 LJ (P. and M.) 62.
7. [1973] Fam. 72.
8. The importance of maintenance for a 'guilty' wife with a child was recognized in *Clear* v. *Clear* [1958] 1 WLR 467, at p. 473, when Hodson LJ said: 'It could hardly be said here that she is entitled to nothing because she has to make a home for the child.'
9. *Report of the Committee on Statutory Maintenance Limits* (1968), (Cmnd. 3587), para. 179.
10. See *Report from His Majesty's Commissioners for Inquiring into the Administration and Practical Operation of the Poor Law* (1834), 44, xxvii, p. 350.
11. (1968), Cmnd. 3587, para. 172.
12. (1968), Cmnd. 3587, para. 96.
13. [1954] P. 41.
14. [1961] P. 16. The same point holds for maintenance ordered by the divorce courts to be paid to a spouse for the upkeep of a child: 'As a matter of construction . . . the scheme of the order is not at all to create an income to which the infant is in any way entitled. The scheme of the order is to increase the income of the mother so as to enable her to discharge the duty of maintenance laid upon her by the court in view of her having the infant's custody' (*Stevens (Inspector of Taxes)* v. *Tizard* [1940] 1 KB 204 at p. 213).
15. *Starke* v. *Starke (No. 2)* [1954] 1 WLR 98 at p. 103, per Lord Merriman P; *Naylor* v. *Naylor* [1962] P. 253. The problem could be overcome by making an application under the Guardianship of Infants Act 1925.
16. Ibid.
17. [1964] P. 152.
18. *Vaughan* v. *Vaughan* [1965] P. 15; *Northrop* v. *Northrop* [1967] 2 All ER 961 at p. 966, per Willmer LJ.
19. [1966] 3 All ER 797 (DC); [1967] 2 All ER 961 (CA).
20. [1967] 2 All ER 961 at p. 979.
21. Maintenance Orders Act 1968.
22. (1977) 121 Sol. Jo. 663.
23. Finance Act 1944, s. 25.
24. Income Tax (Small Maintenance) Order, SI 1980 No. 951.
25. *Rayden on Divorce* (6th edn, 1953), p. 566. One hundred and fifty pounds a year was then the lower tax threshold.
26. Matrimonial Proceedings and Property Act 1970, s. 6 (6).
27. Ss. 11 (2), 50 (1).
28. *Practice Direction* [1977] 3 All ER 942.
29. See *Practice Direction* [1983] 2 All ER 679, providing a form of order for payment of school fees. In order to obtain tax advantage, the order may be expressed to be *payable to the child*, but it is then important that the school enters into a contract *with the child, not the parent*. In *Morley-Clarke* v. *Jones* [1985] 1 All ER 31, the court permitted

an order for maintenance to be paid *for* a child to be retrospectively varied to an order for payment *direct to* the child, thus bringing about a tax advantage to the taxpayer with respect to maintenance already paid. No reference was made to any investigation into whether the child maintenance already paid had in fact directly benefitted the child.

30. *Yates* v. *Starkey* [1951] ch. 465.
31. For a full discussion, see Jennifer Levin (1978), 'Direct Maintenance Payments to Children', 8 *Family Law*, 195–8.
32. *J.* v. *KMP Ltd.* [1975] 1 All ER 1030.
33. [1981] AC 1025.
34. Family Income Supplements Act 1970, s. 4 (1).
35. SI 1980/1437, reg. 2 (6).
36. Previously the wife was only under this obligation if she owned separate property: Married Women's Property Act 1890, s. 13.
37. National Assistance Act 1948, s. 42 (1).
38. Supplementary Benefits Act 1976, s. 17 (1).
39. [1952] 2 QB 648.
40. [1955] 2 QB 506.
41. In 1983, only 679 new orders were applied for against fathers with respect to their liability towards their separated wives or legitimate children: *Social Security Statistics 1984*, Supplementary Benefit: Table 34.93 (London, HMSO).
42. *McBurnie (HM Inspector of Taxes* v. *Tacey* (1984) 14 Family Law 247.
43. *Report of the Committee on One-Parent Families* (1974) Cmnd. 5629, vol. 1, pp. 316–7.

3. The Search for New Principles

I. The Movement for Reform

Debates about divorce immediately before and immediately after the Second World War revolved mainly around the scope of the grounds on which divorce should be allowed. A campaign championed by A. P. Herbert[1] successfully resulted in those grounds being widened in England and Wales by the Matrimonial Causes Act 1937. The problems of divorce were perceived to lie either in the laxity of morals which an easier climate of divorce would bring (and, especially in the United States, had brought) about or, alternatively, in the unhappiness caused by the restrictions and anomalies of the prevailing law.[2] The economic hardship resulting from family breakdown was not a significant factor in the debate. The Royal Commission which reviewed the state of the divorce law in England and Scotland from 1951 to 1955, gave relatively little space to the problem of post-divorce maintenance in their final Report.[3] 'A number of witnesses', they reported, 'suggested that the effect of the present law is to encourage a wife to live in idleness for the rest of her life on the maintenance paid by her husband, or former husband.' Some witnesses:

> considered a complete change of principle to be necessary — each spouse should primarily be liable to support himself or herself. It was contemplated, however, that the wife should still be able to apply for maintenance from her husband (or former husband) but the burden would be upon her to satisfy the court that she could not support herself, for instance because her age or ill-health prevented her from working, or because she had young children to look after; it might also be reasonable to allow her maintenance while she was training to take up work.

Other witnesses thought the court should 'take into consideration to a far greater extent than it does at present in fact that the wife, though not working at the time of the application, may well be capable of earning her own living'. Some witnesses suggested that maintenance orders should be of limited duration, others that no 'guilty' wife should be entitled to apply. A number of witnesses thought that a husband should be able to apply on the same terms as a wife.[4]

While recognizing that over the past one hundred years there had been a considerable change in the economic position of married women, the Commission asserted that most married women still looked to the husband as the main breadwinner, and accordingly felt that there should be no material change in the principles relating to maintenance, and endorsed the view that it should be left to the courts to decide what was reasonable. They did, however, think that a wife's potential earning capacity should be taken into account, and that she should be made, in principle, equally liable with the husband. What is of particular interest about the evidence given to the Commission is, first, that none of it was grounded on any information about how the economic effects of divorce were in fact distributed betwen the adults and the children. Secondly, we again see the social perception of the divorced woman as irresponsible and the man as the victim. The year after the Commission's report was published, it was subjected to a devastating critique by O. R. McGregor in *Divorce in England: A Centenary Study* (1957). Only the five concluding pages of this work considered the question of post-divorce maintenance: but there McGregor wrote:

> If the community permits divorce it must be prepared to meet the inevitable consequences of divorce. The present system of maintenance, and the methods by which it is enforced, is a jumble of ad hoc expedients, capriciously assembled during the last hundred years. When the needs of justice require that citizens should have a sure knowledge of their responsibilities and rights, there exists uncertainty and legal and administrative chaos productive of much unnecessary and futile suffering.[5]

McGregor was certainly aware of the fragile factual base of commonly accepted views of the problems of divorced people. In 1956 William Goode published his pioneering study of divorced women in Detroit.[6] His analysis of the post-divorce economic circumstances of these women may be summarized in his comment that 'the divorced wife receives relatively little property from the split of joint possessions, is given very little child support, and in two-fifths of the cases does not receive this support regularly'.[7] Remarriage was the most significant event to affect the women's post-divorce economic lives. In the United Kingdom, a small fragment of a soundly based social picture was constructed by Dennis Marsden in 1969. *Mothers Alone* reports interviews carried out in 1965 and 1966 with 116 mothers living alone with their children and drawing national assistance (now known as supplementary benefit). Confined as it was to women officially living in poverty, the study cannot claim to present a balanced account of the whole population of divorced or separated women. Nevertheless it showed how for *these* women the sums of maintenance actually awarded in their favour amounted to only a fraction of the maximum sums then applicable for magistrates' courts orders. Marsden calculated that this averaged out at one-tenth of the maximum.[8] His study also uncovered a series of anomolies and injustices in the administration and enforcement of the maintenance laws, especially in their relationship to social security payments.

The potential which the experience of marital breakdown has for causing financial hardship, especially on a woman and children, was recognized by some of the critics of the 1969 divorce law reform. The most notable were Lady Summerskill and the Married Women's Association.[9] These sentiments resulted in the insertion into the new law of a provision that, where the divorce was to be based on the ground that the parties had lived separate and apart for five years or more (even though the respondent objected to the divorce), the court could nevertheless refuse the decree if it thought that 'the dissolution of the marriage will result in grave financial or other hardship to the respondent'.[10] Yet even this solicitude, which is extended only to the 'respondent' (not the children), is entangled with the moral issues relating to the grounds of divorce, because it only applies where an 'innocent' adult is divorced against his or her will. It does not extend to situations where the divorce is based on the respondent's adultery, desertion, or 'unreasonable behaviour'. As for the children, the court need be satisfied only that the arrangements made for them are 'satisfactory or are *the best that can be devised in the circumstances*'.[11]

Despite this partial recognition of the economic hardships which divorce could cause to women and children, dissatisfaction with the principles of post-divorce maintenance as they had been expounded by the Law Commission in 1969 and incorporated in the reform of 1971[12] centred mainly on its apparent basis in the 'persisting obligation' theory. The obligations of marriage, it was claimed, were being perpetuated after its dissolution.[13] This, as we have argued in Chapter 1, misreads the history of the matter. The basis on which post-divorce maintenance was originally awarded did not rest on a simple projection beyond divorce of an existing marital obligation. The courts were more concerned to protect the public purse, shield women from 'temptation' and, most of all, deter against irresponsible rejection of marriage vows. However, in so far as the principles were founded on moral disapproval of divorce, the critics correctly perceived their inconsistency with the emerging no-fault basis of divorce law. Other critics echoed the fears of some of the witnesses to the 1951–6 Royal Commission that awards were being made which were unfair to divorced men and encouraged women to live in idleness.

Largely as a result of these pressures,[14] less than ten years after the introduction of the reformed law of maintenance in 1971, the Lord Chancellor asked the Law Commission to reconsider the whole question. This the Commission did in its discussion paper published in 1980, *The Financial Consequences of Divorce: The Basic Policy*.[15] The Commission observed that the courts had been inconsistent in their application of the 'persisting obligation' principle, pointing especially to decisions relating to short marriages, where some appeared openly to reject the theory, despite its statutory force.[16] Research had shown that registrars, through whom the jurisdiction is exercised in the overwhelming majority of cases, adopted divergent attitudes to the principle, many considering it impracticable.[17] The major weakness of the law lay in the structure of the controlling statutory provision. For, although it proclaimed the principle as the ultimate goal of financial adjustment, it at the same time qualified this by subjecting it to the courts' consideration of other factors, in the light of which they were to assess the justice of its application. It was not, therefore, difficult for the principle to be displaced by other principles according to an individual judge's (or registrar's) sense of justice. No clear judicial guidance was given on the relative weight to be given to these factors, with the exception of the direction of the Court of Appeal that matrimonial misconduct was to be considered relevant only in the most extreme cases.[18] Hence, a review of the cases in 1979 suggested that the persisting obligation principle was being replaced by the objective that primacy was to be given to meeting the needs of the children,[19] with a principle of compensation playing an uncertain and subsidiary role. A later review detected the abandonment of all principle in this area, and argued that the cases could be classified into three groups according to the wealth of the parties. In the most and least wealthy cases the courts rejected the principle, in the latter because they could do no more than attempt to 'meet basic needs' and in the former because this would be 'unrealistic'. In the middle range of cases the courts could achieve more than meeting basic needs, and adopted some version of the one-third rule.[20]

Contemporaneously with the growing dissatisfaction expressed in England on the principles of granting post-divorce maintenance, new sets of principles were emerging in other common law jurisdictions. The Australian Family Law Act 1975[21] permitted maintenance to be ordered 'if and only if' the applicant is 'unable to support herself or himself adequately whether by reason of having the care and control of a child of the marriage who has not attained the age of eighteen years, or by reason of age or physical or mental incapacity for gainful employment or for any other adequate reason'. In 1976 the Law Reform Commission of Canada proclaimed that:

> marriage *per se* should not create a right to receive or an obligation to make financial provision after dissolution; a formerly married person should be responsible for himself or herself' and that the right to financial provision should be created by reasonable needs flowing from the division of functions in marriage, the express or tacit understanding of the spouses that one will make financial provision for the other, custodial arrangements made with respect to the children of the marriage, the physical or mental disability of either spouse that affects his or her ability to provide for himself or herself, or the inability of a spouse to obtain gainful employment.[22]

Since that time, provincial legislatures in Canada have been active in refashioning the maintenance obligation according to such principles[23] but, for constitutional reasons, they can do so only with regard to separations falling short of divorce. Nevertheless, there is evidence that this policy is affecting the way maintenance is being ordered under the federal Divorce Act,[24] although the practice seems inconsistent.[25]

In Britain, too, the Scottish Law Commission issued a Memorandum[26] in 1976 putting forward a different principle for financial adjustment on divorce: 'Financial provision on divorce should not be based in the principle that there is a continuing alimentary relationship between the parties. Rather, its purpose should be to adjust equitably the economic advantages and disadvantages arising from the marriage, in so far as this adjustment is not made by other branches of law.'[27] This principle was fully developed in the Commission's final report in 1981.[28] New Zealand altered its maintenance law in 1981, confining the maintenance obligation after divorce to where it is necessary to meet the 'reasonable needs' of that other party if that party cannot meet those needs, due to the effects of the division of functions within the marriage while the parties were living together, any custodial arrangements regarding the children, or one party undergoing education or training designed to reduce that party's need for maintenance from the other.[29] In the United States the tone of the 1970s had been set by the Uniform Marriage and Divorce Act of 1970, which confined the award of maintenance to cases where the applicant spouse lacked sufficient property to provide for his reasonable needs and was 'unable to support himself through appropriate employment or is the custodian of a child whose condition or circumstances make it appropriate that the custodian not be required to seek employment outside the home'.[30] Writing in 1976, Glendon observed that,

> the principal trends in spousal maintenance after divorce are to equalize the rights of husbands and wives and at the same time to limit maintenance to a temporary period and to cases of genuine need. Even in cases where support is required, the trend is to favour an award that will enable the non-self-sufficient spouse to become self-sufficient, rather than to provide maintenance for life.[31]

II. The Five Models

Apart from the options of retaining the principle of the persisting obligation or of repealing it without offering further guidance, the Law Commission, in its 1980 Discussion Paper, put forward five models on which post-divorce adjustment could be based: (a) The relief of need; (b) Rehabilitation; (c) The division of property — the 'clean break'; (d) A mathematical approach; and (e) Restoration of the parties to the position in which they would have been had their marriage never taken place. They also noted that a combination of models might be thought appropriate.

(a) The relief of need

The concept of 'need' has been at the basis of most of the new departures in recasting the maintenance obligation. For example, section 15 of the Ontario Family Law Reform Act 1978[32] enacts that 'every spouse has an obligation to provide support for himself or herself and for the other spouse, in accordance with need, to the extent that he or she is capable of doing so'.[33] The New Zealand legislation, as we have seen, confines the maintenance obligation to the extent necessary to meet 'reasonable needs' of the other party which arise in a specified way.[34] The Australian formulation restricts the maintenance obligation to circumstances where one party 'is unable to support herself or himself adequately'.[35] Yet, as the Law Commission pointed out[36] and has been recognized elsewhere,[37] the concept is not free from difficulty and requires further working out.

An immediate problem arises where the former spouse is in receipt of state benefits which are, at least in principle, designed to provide for his or her 'needs'. In such a case, is there any room, on the 'needs' principle, for the other spouse to provide additional support? Normally, however, what counts as 'needs' is determined by reference to the claimant's former standard of living.[38] This was how the common law interpreted the idea of 'necessaries', but this could slide into a revival of the 'persisting obligation' theory.[39] If, on the other hand, the payments do not exceed the amounts received by way of state support, the issue resolves into whether the cost of shielding a former spouse from poverty should fall on the former partner or on the state. It is not immediately clear on what theory state poverty programmes towards adult individuals should be alleviated by a divorced spouse, unless entry into marriage is viewed as undertaking some kind of long-term commitment to do this. The poor law did not, and modern social security law does not, treat a divorced spouse as liable to recompense the state for its support of his (or her) former spouse. But the English judges applying private maintenance law have taken the view that a divorced husband should relieve the state of this burden, so far as he can.[40] The Australian Family Law Act, however, requires the eligibility of either party to any state benefit to be taken into acount when a court considers liability to maintain after divorce,[41] but this requirement conflicts with the expectation of Australian social security legislation that a deserted wife will have taken reasonable steps to obtain maintenance. This has led to divergent judicial decisions.[42] The New Zealand Family Proceedings Act 1980 specifically retains a person's liability to maintain another, notwithstanding that the claimant's 'reasonable needs' are being met by a 'domestic benefit'.[43] Such benefits are mostly payable in circumstances connected with child caregiving, in which case the state has a right of recourse against the liable parent,[44] so that public and private law are in harmony; in some cases, however, 'domestic purposes' benefit is payable where there is no right of recourse (as where a woman over fifty loses the support of her husband after a lengthy marriage), in which case the persistence of the private law obligation, where the state is 'meeting needs', is incongruous.

An approach based on needs has, furthermore, to decide whether the circumstances creating the needs are of any relevance. The most obvious case is where the necessitous circumstances are brought about by events subsequent to the divorce and unconnected with it. The Australian legislation expressly permits subsequent, unconnected, events to found entitlement because the liability to maintain can arise with respect to a former spouse whose lack of ability for self-support arises 'by reason of age or physical or mental incapacity for appropriate gainful employment'.[45] In New Zealand, on the other hand, the circumstances must be 'marriage related'[46] because the legislation states that the claimant's inability to meet his or her needs must be causally related to the effects of the 'division of functions within the marriage while the parties lived together' or 'any custodial arrangements' made after their separation or his or her entering education or training where, because of the effects of the first two matters or the earlier contribution by the applicant towards the other spouse's education or training, it would be unfair to place the costs of such education or training entirely on the applicant.[47]

Failure to relate subsequently arising needs to the circumstances of the marriage seems to retain a former spouse's role as insurer of his or her divorced partner. It was for this reason that the Scottish Law Commission, as a matter of principle, inclined to reject the persistence of any obligation in favour of a former spouse who fell on evil days subsequent to the marriage. But the Commission commented, 'it is essential that any system should be acceptable to public opinion and it is clear from the comments we have received that many people would find it hard to accept a system which cut off, say, an elderly or disabled spouse with no more than a three year allowance after divorce, no matter how wealthy the other party might be'. The Commission therefore proposed a 'long-stop' provision allowing maintenance to be ordered in favour of a former spouse who would suffer grave financial hardship as a result of the divorce. But this would only cover cases where the conditions giving rise to the hardship existed at the time of the divorce (e.g. illness or disability), not where they occurred subsequent to it. The Commission realized that there would be some artificiality in drawing this line, but considered that 'a line has to be drawn somewhere and that the right place to draw the line is at the date when the legal relationship between the parties comes to an end. After that each should be free to make a new life without liability for future misfortunes which may befall the other'.[48] The New Zealand provisions, however, seem to exclude maintenance even in the case of a former spouse whose earning capacity has been gravely impaired as a result of illness or accident before the divorce, for in such a case the inability to meet needs cannot be said to arise from the circumstances specified in the Act (division of functions within marriage; custodial arrangements). While the New Zealand approach may appear more logical, the result is clearly not uncontroversial. Nor does the requirement of attributing the claimant's needs to 'the division of functions' within marriage always point to clear solutions. Would the abandonment by a wife of a prospective career in order to accompany her husband if he moves in the course of his employment or in order to obtain employment be so attributable? And in any case, is it obviously more appropriate for a former husband to act as insurer for a former wife who during the marriage voluntarily abandoned employment and enjoyed a luxurious lifestyle at his expense, than for a woman who continued to work during the marriage, contributing to the parties' common well-being, but who later suffered physical or financial misfortune?

Some of the most difficult problems concerning the 'needs' approach arise, however, with regard to its relationship to the principle of self-sufficiency. Legislation frequently couples the 'needs' principle with an express direction demanding that each former spouse should seek to attain self-sufficiency, at least as soon as this is reasonable. Thus New Zealand directs that 'where a marriage is dissolved, each party shall assume responsibility, within a period of time that is reasonable in all the circumstances of the particular case, for meeting the party's own needs . . .'.[49] Many Canadian provincial statutes enact the same policy.[50] Where this is not expressly enacted, it has been imported by interpretation. For example, although the Canadian Divorce Act[51] does not expressly refer to this issue, the failure of a former spouse to seek employment can be regarded as a 'material change in circumstances' justifying reduction in maintenance.[52] Similarly, it has been pointed out in Australia that courts may consider post-divorce behaviour which is thought unreasonably to weaken a former spouse's financial position as misconduct which could effect the maintenance entitlement.[53]

The drive for self-sufficiency raises some acute problems. The most usual concern conflict with the calls upon a former spouse who has the care of a child or children. It is probable, as Atkin maintains, that the New Zealand postponement of the self-sufficiency imperative during a 'reasonable' time will include the period of dependency of children, especially children of pre-school age,[54] and that this will be a common view. However, it may not go unchallenged. A Canadian judge has remarked that he took the self-sufficiency principle 'to mean that unless there are valid health or psychological reasons that the mother should remain in the home, the mother is required to hire a baby-sitter or place the child in day-care and resume her former employment or its equivalent'.[55] Another potential conflict between the principle and the children's interests was resolved against the children in *Stere* v. *Stere*.[56]

The former wife had abandoned her full-time employment in favour of part-time work at a private school in return for which her children qualified for free tuition. This arrangement was held to disentitle her to maintenance because she had adopted 'an attitude to employment which cannot be considered in keeping with the obligations cast upon women in this society under the Divorce Act and indeed as recognized in the Family Law Reform Act 1980, that she is obligated to provide support for herself'.[57]

The principle in any case encounters many practical problems in its application. Is it, for example, to be expected that a former wife (perhaps with care of children) who cannot (reasonably) obtain full-time employment should seek part-time work to reduce her dependency? In *Dieter* v. *Dieter*[58] the Ontario Court of Appeal held that a 54-year old wife, who suffered ill-health, should not, after a 25-year marriage during which she was withdrawn form the labour market, be obliged 'to only obtain continued support in the event that she has made every effort to establish herself and provide for herself by her own efforts'. The decision is, however, criticized by the editor of the Reports of Family Law as being inconsistent with the self-sufficiency principle of the Family Law Reform Act 1980. 'She could' he observes, 'perhaps obtain part-time sales or clerical work . . . in difficult economic times any saving of expense is useful'. Yet, as our research has shown, the marginal benefits over subsistence of part-time work for women may be very narrow, if detectable at all.[59] It is unclear to what kinds of savings the comment refers. If they are those of the husband (who in that case was relatively affluent) the reference to 'difficult economic times' seems obscure. If they are those of the state, the issue becomes one not of the justice of the private maintenance obligation but of the state's policy towards welfare and employment.

Apart from the difficulties surrounding the economic value of part-time work (for the worker), the self-sufficiency principle encounters the practical difficulties of assessing the availability of employment in specific areas. Sometimes courts have appeared to assume without apparent enquiry that work is easily available.[60] Should evidence on this matter be presented to the court? Where work is unavailable locally, should the applicant be required to leave accustomed surroundings in order to seek it?[61] Should the applicant accept *any* employment, irrespective of the nature of his or her previous work experience or training?[62] And what policy should be adopted if the applicant is deterred from seeking employment because she is caring for children who are not those of her former partner, or if she is caring for a disabled or handicapped relative (e.g. her mother)?[63] But a fundamental problem remains unsolved by the 'needs' principle. Are a spouse's (or children's) 'reasonable needs' satisfied if they are supported by state funds at subsistence level or by earnings a little above that? If not, and if the qualification 'reasonable' implies reference to their former condition, at what level are they satisfied? These questions form the major subject matter of Chapters 7 and 8.

(b) Rehabilitation

The goal of rehabilitation is another way of expressing the self-sufficiency principle. It allows for limited post-divorce support while a former partner attempts to recover the ability to support himself or herself. As such it encounters the problems discussed above in relation to the self-sufficiency principle. But rehabilitation could hardly stand alone as a basis for post-divorce support. A person may (due to illness, age, or some other reason) be incapable of achieving self-support, or may fail to achieve it due to external causes (such as economic recession). Success may be impeded by the exercise of child care. It would be hard to see why support should be provided only so far as self-sufficiency is being sought, but denied when it is unattainable.[64] Furthermore, as Atkin points out, rehabilitative support alone may fail to compensate a former spouse for losses incurred by entering marriage.[65] Indeed, the expression itself implies some form of restoration of a status quo ante. In some cases it may not be so much a question of restoring a former spouse to self-support, but introducing him or her to this state. Yet the requirement to achieve self-sufficiency would presumably apply none the less for that. It seems, therefore, that the concept of rehabilitation in effect collapses into one aspect of the principle of needs.

(c) The division of property — the 'clean break'

As the Law Commission stated, the essence of this model is the analogy of partnership: that property should be divided (equally or otherwise) and that should be the end of the matter.[66] This was the fundamental position of the Scottish Law Commission, which took the view that an order for continuing maintenance should not be made unless capital sum payments or property reallocation failed to give effect to their proposed principles of financial adjustment.[67] The Australian Family Law Act 1975 expresses the same policy in section 81, which urges courts, so far as practicable, to 'make such orders as will finally determine the financial relationships between the parties to the marriage and avoid further proceedings between them'. This, it has been suggested, has led courts to prefer lump sum or property orders over provisions for continuing maintenance.[68]

There are really two points at issue under this heading. One is whether the distribution of property should be effected entirely in accordance with 'property based' concepts, with no account taken of the needs either partner may have in the future; in other words, should it be *solely* a matter of 'settling accounts'? The other point is whether, given that future needs are a relevant consideration, an attempt should be made to provide for them once and for all at the time of divorce, with the opportunities for future legal proceedings effectively cut out? The points will be considered separately.

(i) A settling of accounts

That there should be some element of asset distribution relating to their mode of acquisition during the marriage in any divorce settlement seems undeniable. Until recently in England and Wales the law of property and of trusts has borne the major impact of the growth of this policy imperative. Cases arose, especially after the Second World War, in which a marriage broke down at a time when the major capital asset (the home) had appreciated considerably in value but remained in the legal ownership of one spouse (invariably, the husband), despite the fact that the wife may have contributed to its purchase under mortgage by contributing her earnings to the household budget.[69] Lacking, before 1971, any general powers of redistributing property on divorce, the courts used the device of the resulting (or constructive) trust in order to carve out for such a wife a beneficial interest in the value of the property, which would fall into her hands when it was sold. But the courts were careful to limit the circumstances where such an interest could be acquired to those amounting to *more* than ordinary household work.[70] If they had failed to do this, they would effectively have arrogated to themselves the power to distribute property simply on the basis that the parties had been married to each other.

But in 1971 the English courts acquired this very power. In making orders for financial provision, which might include transferring property and lump sums, the courts were permitted to 'have regard', among other things, to 'the contributions made by each of the parties to the welfare of the family, including any contribution made by looking after the home or caring for the family'.[71] In recommending this extension, the Law Commission sought to meet the criticism that the existing law failed adequately to compensate a wife for her 'domestic' services.[72] There are, however, extensive difficulties in taking this approach. How is one to evaluate, in economic terms, such 'contributions'? Is the homemaker's contribution to be assessed in terms of her own economic deprivation ('opportunity costs') or the costs such services could have been acquired commercially ('replacement costs')?[73] How far is it right to evaluate the efficiency of the role performance or the motives whereby it was undertaken?[74]

Gray has pointed out that the attempt to place a monetary value on a homemaker's (or child caregiver's) contributions commits the 'cardinal error of applying exchange criteria to what is essentially a use value'. To allow a wife a share in the *husband*'s property as compensation for such contributions is essentially to view marriage as a contractual exchange for the wife's services.[75] It was for reasons such as these that many legislatures (and the Scottish Law Commission) have resorted to the principle of equality as a basis for property division on divorce, not as an attempt to reflect 'economic' values of the respective contributions, but as an ideological norm of the marriage partnership.[76] It is important that the ideological basis of this movement should be recognized. Gray, for example, asserts that the rule of equality 'unequivocally declares the social ethics at the root of the law'.[77] In effect, the law is imposing on married persons the expectations that capital accumulated during their period of (married) family living should accrue to their respective benefit equally. During marriage, the capital gains of each adult are deemed to be acquired, not individually, but by each adult as an agent for other family members.[78]

Although English law has not adopted this principle, its popularity requires explanation. It represents a high degree of intrusion into economic ordering within families. We would expect to account for this by reference to a perceived discordance between assumptions about how such ordering should take place within families and how it does so in fact. When the discrepancy becomes sufficiently threatening, the reaction can be either to abandon the normative image entirely or to attempt to impose it by legal means. It is probable, therefore, that the latter course was adopted in the face of the growing instability of middle class families as divorce became progressively within their reach. Thus, the principle of equal division of assets on dissolution coupled with protection against the dispersal of family assets during the marriage, was first clearly established in the Scandinavian countries during the first quarter of this century.[79] These reforms had been preceded by the introduction of relatively liberal divorce laws in those countries.[80] The reception of the Scandinavian deferred community scheme in the common law world occurred alongside the rapid increase in divorce following the Second World War. The liberalization of divorce was contemporaneous with an increase in the economic activity of women and it may be that the two phenomena are related. It may be concluded that it was the prospect of women *losing* what were deemed the proper fruits of their efforts on marriage breakdown which provided the incentive for legal intervention.

However attractive the norm of equality appears, the use of law to impose an ideology of family living must always attract close scrutiny. We must ask from where the ideology derives and what are the consequences of its imposition. It is probable that the origins of the principle are to be found in the same ethic which sustains modern commitments to democracy and equality. This ideology seems to have spilled over from the political and social arenas into the functioning of family life.[81] Each adult's contribution should be regarded as being of equal value, entitling equal economic rewards. Research has frequently shown the prevalence of the assumption among married people that they have a common interest in their property acquisitions.[82] But this information should be treated with care. The same research also shows that most married people have very little accumulated capital. Those who are committed to the partnership ideology are prepared to press its application to investments, business (and agricultural) property (including goodwill), pensions, job security, and sometimes, even earning capacity.[83] It is not at all clear how far these extensions would be reflected in the general consensus, particularly on the part of individuals likely to be significantly affected by them. Furthermore, the research indicated that a distinction was made between childless couples and those with children. In Scotland, it was found that over half the people surveyed thought that the law should allocate more of the family property to the parent with the custody of the children.[84]

But the most significant challenge to viewing adjustment on divorce solely in terms of a settling of accounts, whether reached by application of a norm of equality or otherwise, lies in difficulty in reconciling the results reached by this method with competing principles relating to the claims of family members, particularly the children. In California, the introduction of no-fault divorce by the Family Law Act 1969 was accompanied by the imposition of a norm of equal sharing of matrimonial property. Formerly, property adjustments were linked to assessments of relative fault. In comparing the property dispositions made by California courts under the new law with those made under the old, Weitzman[85] found, first, that most divorcing couples have little or no property to divide;[86] second, that before the reform, where property division was recorded, in most cases the larger share went to the wife. After the change, the proportion of wives receiving the greater part of the property fell drastically in favour of equal division. This trend applied to the family home as well as to other items of property. The apparent equity of this trend becomes questionable when it is appreciated that it is most likely that any children of the marriage will remain with the wife after divorce. The former wife's family unit is (unless the husband reconstitutes a new family) usually larger than that of the former husband. The equal division between adults is not, therefore, an equal division *between all family members*. It takes no account of household composition. This point is of particular importance in regard to the house. For if, as seems likely, equal division frequently compels the sale of the house, the use of that asset for the benefit of the child members of the family is frustrated.[87] In so far as independent arguments may be made on behalf of the children, which we will develop later, the view of property adjustment as no more than a distribution between the adults appears too narrow.

(ii) A once-and-for-all settlement

It may be conceded that more is at stake in divorce settlement than merely winding up a partnership between adults, but nevertheless contended that policy should promote the resolution of these matters in a once-and-for-all settlement. This view is partly based on the rejection of the idea that support obligations should persist after divorce. That a support matter might be reopened after divorce is plainly inconsistent with the principle that all obligations between the spouses cease when the marriage finishes. To this is added the psychological claim that it is better for the adults 'to put the past behind them and to begin a new life which is not overshadowed by the relationship which has broken down'.[88] This policy would, it is argued, contribute to the contentment of the second marriages which is said to be undermined by the persistent diversion of their resources towards the former family and even the continued threat of renewed claims from that quarter.[89]

Whether all obligations between spouses should terminate on divorce is one of the questions under discussion in this book. At this point it need be noted only that if any claim is permitted to a former spouse even on the limited principle of needs (or some equivalent), *such a claim would only arise on divorce* and, if recognized, would defeat the principle that all obligations cease on divorce. Apart from that point, it is usually conceded that obligations regarding children do survive divorce,[90] and are commonly enforced on their behalf by the caregiving parent. That there may be such obligations relating to the time after divorce does not necessarily, of course, mean that procedural means cannot be devised to achieve their discharge in advance by, for example, a property transfer or lump sum payment. But until we have settled whether there *should* be any post-divorce obligations and, if so, what they should be, this issue should be deferred.

(d) A mathematical approach

The Law Commission drew attention to some suggestions that post-divorce support should be settled as far as possible by a mathematically-precise code.[91] The Commission compared this suggestion to the one-third 'rule', sometimes used by the courts, more usually as a 'guide' or 'starting point' rather than a 'precise code'. The difficulty with such a code, in the Commission's view, was that it lacked the flexibility necessary when dealing with individual cases. Nor, of course, does consideration of such a code in itself resolve the fundamental questions such as whether there should be any post-divorce support obligation at all, or, if so, what its purpose should be. However, once the principal objectives of post-divorce support are settled, it may be possible to find formulae which can adequately translate them into practice. The Law Commission's second report on the matter, in which it recommended the principle of priority for the needs of children, came close to recognizing this.[92] The Commission observed that the courts should have 'adequate data about the actual costs of providing for the needs of children'. However, the mere provision of such data would not in itself provide guidance as to how these costs should be met. Another approach would be to construct some formula which would determine the proportion of the debtor's resources which should be available for the support of the children. This is a common feature of systems which guarantee a level of child support from the state funds with a right of recourse against the liable relative, and is under active consideration in the United States, where amendments to the federal child suport enforcement legislation, enacted in 1984, require states to produce 'standards' for child support awards by 1986.[93] Principles relevant to this issue will be examined in Chapter 7.

(e) Restoration of the status quo ante

Gray has argued that the true objective of financial adjustment should be 'to replace the parties in the position which would have occurred had the marriage never taken place'.[94] The Law Commission rejected this on the grounds that it would involve unsatisfactory speculation about what might have happened had the parties not married each other.[95] Apart from this objection, it must be clear that in many cases especially if children have been born, the parties cannot be restored to that original position. Nevertheless, the idea was taken up, in somewhat different form, by the Scottish Law Commission when it proposed that one of the principles upon which adjustment on divorce should be based should be 'fair recognition of contributions and disadvantages'. The Commission pointed out that a spouse may have sustained economic disadvantage on entering marriage, and that some recompense for this should be reflected in any award.[96] While there seems to be a straightforward case in justice for the recognition of such a claim, if demonstrated, severe problems would result unless its scope of application were to be narrow. If, for example, a woman abandons a career, marries, has children and devotes her time to caring for them, is she to be compensated by her husband *for her career loss* if the marriage later collapses? The Scottish Commission seemed to think she should.[97] This is to equate a voluntary decision in favour of child rearing with tortious injury. At the very least, any such economic loss should be in principle offset against the benefits of producing and raising children, arguably an impossible calculation.[98] This seems to confirm our scepticism about the feasibility of applying restitutory principles in cases where children have been born. However, in childless cases, it may be more readily perceived that the husband has directly benefited from his wife's economic sacrifice, and the compensatory principle be applied.

III. The Matrimonial and Family Proceedings Act 1984

Having received representations on the basis of the Discussion Paper, and taking into account public debate on these questions, the Law Commission produced a set of recommendations in 1981.[99] There was overwhelming support for the rejection of the persisting obligation theory. In its place, the Commission suggested that legislation should 'embody the principle that the interests of the children should be seen as a matter of overriding importance'.[100] Within the context of this overarching objective, greater weight should be given to the 'importance of each party doing everything possible to become self-sufficient' and, wherever possible, a once-and-for-all settlement should be achieved. Beyond this, the Commission thought that 'conduct' should still play a part in the determination of post-divorce support, but its elaboration would best be left to the courts, and that courts should continue to be entitled to take into account the contributions of a second spouse to the payer's total resources in determining what would be an appropriate sum for him to pay his former spouse.[101]

In 1982, a private member's bill was introduced into the House of Commons with the object of giving legislative effect to the policy embodied in the Law Commission document.[102] The bill failed on the dissolution of Parliament, but in 1983 a new version was introduced into the House of Lords as a government measure. Its passage was marked by an intense conflict between those who continued to maintain, as had the witnesses to the Royal Commission of 1951–6, that the persisting obligation principle inflicted serious injustice on maintenance payers (men) and on their new families, and other groups who advanced the more recently acquired perception that women and children were the chief victims of the economic hardships of divorce.[103] In the event, the Act introduced the following changes into the English law of post-divorce maintenance.

The legislation removed the persisting obligation principle, as it applied with respect to post-divorce support between the adults and to post-divorce support for children. In its place is found the proclamation that, in making financial provision on divorce, the court is to have regard to all the circumstances of the case, 'first consideration being given to the welfare while a minor of any child of the family who has not attained the age of eighteen'.[104] We shall consider the implication of this principle in detail in Chapter 7. At this point we would observe, first, that the expression 'first consideration' has been interpreted as meaning something different from 'overriding' or 'priority' consideration,[105] which is what the Law Commission intended.[106] If this weaker interpretation is accepted, the enactment will do little more than express the presently proclaimed view that the interests of the children are of the greatest importance. If, on the other hand, the stronger interpretation is adopted, the result will be to give priority to the children of the first marriage over any children for whom the payer may subsequently become responsible. This is probably contrary to practice preceding the Act, which, at least in cases concerning parties of moderate means, seemed to aim at achieving an equivalence between the final net incomes of the two family groups.[107] Apart from these difficulties, the Act says no more on the question, leaving it entirely to the courts to determine how this principle is to be translated into practice.

The Act promotes the self-sufficiency principle in a number of ways. It requires the courts not only to take into account the spouses' earning capacity, but also any 'increase in that capacity which it would in the opinion of the court be reasonable to expect a party to the marriage to take steps to acquire'.[108] Before making an order for continuing support, the court is enjoined first to consider whether it would be 'appropriate' to make an order which will have the effect of severing the financial obligations between the parties 'as soon after the grant of the decree as the court considers just and reasonable'. If, having thought about bringing about an immediate 'clean break', the court nevertheless decides to impose a continuing obligation, it must still direct its mind to the question whether it would be 'appropriate to require those payments to be made or secured only for such term as would in the opinion of the court be sufficient to enable the party in whose favour the order is made to adjust without undue hardship to the termination of his or her financial dependence on the other party'. This issue is also to be considered on application to vary an order for continuing support.[109]

The repeated use of the expression 'appropriate' indicates the extent of the discretion which remains with the court. It may be assumed that the general requirement to place the interests of children of the family first, means that the self-sufficiency principle will not be employed if this would injure those interests. The President of the Family Division, in giving evidence to the Special Standing Committee of the House of Commons which considered the Bill, claimed that the provisions of the Bill in no way altered the powers then available to the courts.[110] In one respect, however, the Act does enhance those powers. Prior to the enactment, a court was able to cut out a divorced spouse's right to return to the court at any time after the divorce and apply for maintenance only if, at the time of the divorce, that spouse consented to this course.[111] To have done so without such consent would have deprived that person of a statutory right. This is changed by the 1984 Act; later applications may be barred without such consent.[112]

IV. Conclusion

We have argued thus far, firstly, that the perception that the 'traditional' law of post-divorce maintenance was founded on the concept that the marital support obligation survived divorce, is historically inaccurate. When, reluctantly, the English courts originally awarded maintenance after granting judicial divorce, this was not founded on a theory of the persistence of the matrimonial obligation, but was for an amalgam of reasons. Partly they sought to restore to the former wife property which the husband had acquired from her on marriage. This motive was diminished by the introduction of general separation of property in 1882. Sometimes they made an award as a solace to the woman or, in more extreme cases, to keep her from poverty or the temptations of vice. Most importantly, they based their awards on the principle that husbands should not lightly depart from their marital vows: they should be penalized for their misconduct. However, during the course of the twentieth century the principle of the persisting obligation took hold, although the legal foundation for this was weak.

With the general introduction of no-fault divorce, the basis on which financial adjustment was carried out required fundamental review. We have examined the main principles which have been advanced for the making of post-divorce awards. None of them, taken alone, has been found to offer a satisfactory foundation for policy in this area. Even the new emphasis in the Matrimonial and Family Proceedings Act 1984 on the welfare of the child remains obscure in its implications. One of the major reasons for this, we suggest, is that the discussions preceding its introduction have taken place at an ideological level, with little reference to information about how the pre-existing systems actually operated. The persisting obligation principle was perceived to rest on an out-dated concept of life-long support, representing the legal dependency of married women, and inconsistent with modern values. The Law Commission expressed its concern about proceeding in the absence of empirical knowledge.[113] Other bodies have been less fastidious. The Working Paper of the Law Reform Commission of Canada, which set out new principles for maintenance awards,[114] made no attempt to discover or present any information about the financial circumstances of divorced families. Nor was any such information available to the Ontario Law Reform Commission,[115] and the Berger Commission in British Columbia relied only on an article in the *Wall Street Journal*.[116] Chisholm and Jessep (1981) observe how, when the Australian reforms of 1975 were proposed, public discussion was confined to the issue of no-fault divorce and that scarcely any attention was paid to the new principles for awarding post-divorce maintenance. Even in the United States,despite Goode's initial work, calls for reform in the law of alimony focussed attention on the inequity of the persisting obligation principle. 'Alimony', wrote Hofstadter and Levithan in 1967,[117] 'was never intended to assure a perpetual state of assured indolence. It should not be suffered to convert a host of physically and mentally competent young women into an army of alimony drones who neither toil nor spin, and become a drain on society and themselves.' No evidence was offered to substantiate this claim. Only after the Uniform Marriage and Divorce Act of 1970 had reset the compass guiding courts in awarding alimony did detailed evidence of the operation of these awards begin to emerge largely as a result of the work in California by Lenore Weitzman.[118] The Scottish Law Commission, however, had the benefit of a survey of orders made in Scottish courts.[119] These data did not, however, reveal the extent to which these orders were carried out, nor did they provide evidence of the relative economic conditions of the families concerned. Nevertheless, when combined with such information as now exists on these matters, the Scottish survey has proved a valuable exercise.

The research reported in later chapters in this book represents an attempt to provide, in England, some factual information against which the new directions in maintenance law can be assessed. It will be our contention that the information throws sufficient new light on the policies and principles under discussion that they require fundamental review. Any such review will confront deep issues of social policy which involve political value judgements. We will not shirk such judgements, but regard it as our primary task to expose where they lie.

Notes

1. B. H. Lee (1974), *Divorce Reform in England* (London, Peter Owen), pp. 16–18.
2. See Chapter 1, n. 35.
3. *Royal Commission on Marriage and Divorce* (1956), (Cmnd. 9678), Part 7.
4. (1956), Cmnd. 9678, paras. 485–90.
5. O. R. McGregor (1957), *Divorce in England: A Centenary Study* (London, Heinemann), p. 196.
6. W. Goode (1956), *After Divorce* (New York, The Free Press), republished in 1965 as *Women in Divorce*. The interviews were carried out in 1948.
7. Goode (1965), p. 222.
8. D. Marsden (1973), *Mothers Alone* (Harmondsworth, Penguin Books), p. 19.
9. See B. H. Lee (1974), pp. 173–5, 201.
10. Matrimonial Causes Act 1973, s. 5 (2).
11. Matrimonial Causes Act 1973, s. 41 (1) (b).
12. Matrimonial Proceedings and Property Act 1970.
13. See Kevin Gray (1977), *The Re-allocation of Property on Divorce* (Abingdon, Professional Books), pp. 282–3, 321, citing, among other sources, a dictum in a New

Jersey court that alimony after divorce 'is simply a continuation of a husband's duty to support his wife and grows out of the marital relationship'; Law Commission (1980), *Family Law: The Financial Consequences of Divorce: The Basic Policy* (Law Com. No. 103, para. 12), describing the obligation as analogous to contract; Scottish Law Commission (1976), *Family Law: Aliment and Financial Provisions*, Memorandum No. 22, vol. 2, para. 3.2.

14. An articulate pressure group, *The Campaign for Justice in Divorce*, putting forward predominantly the grievances of divorced men, arose towards the end of the 1970s and claimed to have persuaded the Lord Chancellor to refer the matter to the Law Commission. See also Law Com. No. 103, para. 1 (acknowledging a 'helpful memorandum from the Campaign for Justice in Divorce'). There are other references to the activity of this pressure group by the Lord Chancellor in 401 HL Deb. col. 1459 (18 July 1979) and 405 HL Deb. col. 148 (12 February 1980). He refers to its success in 'literally pelting' him with letters complaining about the hardships faced by divorced husbands and their second wives.

15. Law Com. No. 103 (1980), Cmnd. 8041.

16. Law Com. No. 103, paras. 61–4. Subsequent to the Law Commission's report, the statutory requirement to apply the theory formed the basis of the Court of Appeal's decision in *Potter* v. *Potter* [1982] 1 WLR 1255 (a childless marriage lasting six years).

17. W. Barrington Baker, John Eekelaar, Colin Gibson and Susan Raikes (1977), *The Matrimonial Jurisdiction of Registrars* (Oxford, SSRC Centre for Socio-Legal Studies).

18. *Wachtel* v. *Wachtel* [1973] Fam. 72.

19. J. M. Eekelaar (1979), 'Some Principles of Financial and Property Adjustment on Divorce', 95 *Law Quarterly Rev.*, 253–69.

20. Ruth Deech (1982), 'Financial Relief: The Retreat from Precedent and Principle', 98 *Law Quarterly Rev.*, 621–55.

21. Family Law Act 1975, s. 72.

22. Law Reform Commission of Canada (1976), *Family Law* (Ottawa, Information Canada), pp. 42–3.

23. See below, p. 38, nn. 32, 33.

24. Divorce Act 1970, c. D–8. See *Mero* v. *Mero* (1983) 32 RFL (2d) 137 (Ont.); *Pearson* v. *Pearson* (1983) WDFL 259.

25. See especially the judgement of the British Columbia Court of Appeal in *Berry* v. *Murray* (1983) 30 RFL (2d) 310.

26. (1976), Memorandum No. 22.

27. Ibid. para. 3.7.

28. Scottish Law Com. (1981), *Family Law: Report on Aliment and Financial Provision*, Scot. Law Com. No. 67.

29. Family Proceedings Act 1980, s. 64.

30. Uniform Marriage and Divorce Act, s. 308 (a) (2).

31. M. A. Glendon (1976), 'Marriage and the State: The Withering away of Marriage', 62 *Virginia LR* 663–706; Gray (1977), pp. 293–9.

32. Now RSO 1980, c. 152.

33. See also Family Law Reform Act 1978, s. 16 (PEI); Family Relations Act, RSBC 1979, c. 121, s. 57 (2).

34. See above, n. 29.

35. See above, pp. 36–7.

36. Law Com. No. 103, para. 72 (i).

37. Richard Chisholm and Owen Jessep (1981), 'Fault and Financial Adjustment under the Family Law Act', 4 *Univ. of NSW Law Journal*, No. 2, 43.

38. See, for example, *Evans* v. *Evans* (1978) 30 FLR 566 (Australia).

39. See the reasoning in *Dean* v. *Dean* [1923]·P. 173 (a case of judicial separation). New Zealand courts are expressly barred from having regard to the standard of living of the common household, when considering what are the 'reasonable needs' of each party: Family Proceedings Act 1980, s. 65 (2).

40. *Hyman* v. *Hyman* [1929] AC 601. See the comments of Sir George Baker P. in *Campbell* v. *Campbell* [1976] Fam. 347: 'I ask myself why should the public (social security) keep his ex-wife whom he, not the public, married, rather than that he should make his fair and proper contribution, whatever the effect may be on him.' In *Peacock* v. *Peacock* [1984] 1 All ER 1069 Booth J. accepted that an order should be made against a husband for maintenance while a divorce suit was pending, even though the state, not the wife, would receive its benefit, because this is what the court would do in making the final order after divorce. The attitudes of registrars to this question have been found to vary: see W. Barringon Baker *et al.* (1977), paras. 2.3–7.

41. Family Law Act 1975, s. 75 (2) (f).

42. Malcolm D. Broun (1981), 'Financial Implications of Family Law', 55 *Australian Law Journal*, 424, contrasting *Wong* v. *Wong* (1976) 2 Fam. LR 11, 159 (where the judge took the view that a former wife in receipt of state benefit could not be said to be self-supporting and that he should not, by dismissing her claim against her former husband, 'adjust the property and incomes so as to create a pension entitlement'), with *Todd* v. *Todd (No. 2)* (1976) FLC 90–008. H. A. Finlay (1979), *Family Law in Australia* (2nd edn). Sydney, Butterworths), p. 225, regards the approach in *Wong* as being 'cautious and responsible'.

43. Family Proceedings Act 1980, s. 62.

44. W. R. Atkin (1981), 'Spousal Maintenance: A New Philosophy?', 9 *NZ Universities Law Rev.* 336, at pp. 338–9.

45. Family Law Act 1975, s. 72; Chisholm and Jessup (1981), 43, p. 53. The same seems to be the case under Canadian legislation: see *Kivac* v. *Kivac* (1982) 28 RFL (2d) 23 (Ont. Co. Ct.).

46. Atkin (1981), p. 346.

47. Family Proceedings Act 1980, s. 64 (1).

48. Scot. Law Com. No. 67 (1981), para. 3.110.

49. Family Proceedings Act 1980, s. 64 (2).

50. For example: Family Maintenance Act 1978, s. 4 (Manitoba): '. . . a spouse has the obligation after separation to take all reasonable steps to become financially independent of the other spouse'; Family Relations Act, RSBC 1979, s. 57 (2) (British Columbia): 'a spouse or former spouse is required to be self sufficient in relation to the other spouse or former spouse'.

51. RSC 1970, c. D–8, s. 11.

52. *Pearson* v. *Pearson* [1983] WDFL 259.

53. Chisolm and Jessep (1981), p. 53.

54. Atkin (1981), p. 347.

55. *Re Moosa and Moosa* (1980) ACWS (2d) 110 (Ont. Co. Ct.).

56. (1982) 28 RFL (2d) 325 (SC Ont.).

57. Per Flinn LJSC at p. 332. See also *Marks* v. *Marks* (1982) 29 RFL (2d) 74 (Man. QB), where Hamilton J. reproved a 61-year-old wife for failing to take the steps

required by statute to make herself financially independent of her separated husband.

58. (1982) 25 RFL (2d) 225.
59. See below, p. 94.
60. See the editor's comments on *Molz* v. *Molz* (1982) 29 RFL (2d) 353 (Ont.); see also *McDiarmid* v. *McDiarmid* (1982) 29 RFL (2d) 132 (Sask.) (maintenance was denied to an out-of-work schoolteacher with a child of eleven, on the ground that she 'ought to be able to find employment'.)
61. The point was left open in *Carlson* v. *Carlson* (1982) 29 RFL (2d) 414 (Sask.).
62. Law Com. No. 103, para. 72 (ii).
63. See Chisholm and Jessup (1981), p. 55, who suggest that the exercise by the applicant of choice regarding post-divorce *family arrangements* should not be considered as conduct prejudicial to the maintenance entitlement.
64. See Law Com. No. 103, para. 76.
65. Atkin (1981), p. 342.
66. Law Com. No. 103, para. 77.
67. Scot. Law Com. No. 67, para. 3.121.
68. Broun (1981), p. 427.
69. The leading cases are *Pettitt* v. *Pettitt* [1970] AC 777 and *Gissing* v. *Gissing* [1970] AC 886. There is considerable controversy over the true jurisdictional basis for these decisions. See generally, John Eekelaar (1984), *Family Law and Social Policy* (London, Weidenfeld and Nicolson), pp. 102–4. Similar doctrines evolved in Canada, for the same reasons: Eekelaar (1984), p. 225.
70. *Murdoch* v. *Murdoch* (1973) 41 DLR (3d) 367 (SC Can.); *Burns* v. *Burns* [1984] 1 All ER 244.
71. Matrimonial Proceedings and Property Act 1970, s. 5 (1) (f); re-enacted as Matrimonial Causes Act 1973, s. 25 (1) (f).
72. Law Commission (1969), *Family Law: Report on Financial Provisions in Matrimonial Proceedings*, Law Com. No. 25.
73. See Harvey Rosen (1974), 'The Monetary Value of a Housewife: A Replacement Cost Approach', *American Journal of Economics and Society*, 65; E. J. Pottick (1978), 'Tort Damages for the Injured Homemaker: Opportunity Cost or Replacement Cost?', 50 *Univ. of Colorado Law Rev.*, 59; and the critical comments by Jack L. Knetsch (1984), 'Some Economic Implications of Matrimonial Property Rules', 34 *Univ. of Toronto Law Journal*, 263–82.
74. See A. Zuckerman (1978), 'Ownership of the Matrimonial Home — Common Sense and Reformist Nonsense', 94 *Law Quarterly Rev.*, 26, at p. 48: 'there is a fundamental difference between a wife who refrains from taking paid employment in order to look after her family and husband, thus enabling the latter to devote greater energy to his career, and a wife who stays away from work merely because she considers herself entitled to be supported, regardless of any contribution on her part to the family welfare'; see also Gray (1977), p. 77.
75. Gray (1977), p. 77.
76. See Gray (1977), ch. 3; also Scot. Law Com. No. 67 (1981), para. 3.67.
77. Gray (1977), p. 115. The norm of equal division does not, however, operate in favour of children. It may be expected that the adults will use their capital holdings (notably, the home) for the benefit of the children, but this is rarely reflected in enforceable legal rights in the children. See generally above, Chapters 1 and 2.
78. This statement requires qualification with respect to continental European

countries which operated community of property systems. Joint ownership of matrimonial assets reflected the social expectation regarding their use. However, the husband was given (virtually) untrammelled power to manage the assets. In such systems, therefore, the legal enforcement of the partnership expectation took the form of growing restrictions upon his power of management of the communal property, particularly if it came from the wife or her family.

79. See A. Malmstrom in W. Friedmann (ed.) (1955), *Matrimonial Property Law* (London, Stevens); Folke Schmidt (1971), 'The Prospective Law of Marriage', *Scandinavian Studies in Law*, 193–218.

80. Svenne Schmidt (1984), 'The Scandinavian Law of Procedure and Matrimonial Causes', in Eekelaar and Katz (eds.), *The Resolution of Family Conflict: Comparative Legal Perspectives* (Toronto, Butterworths), ch. 5.

81. A. J. Manners and I. Rauta (1981), *Family Property in Scotland* (London, HMSO), p. 22; Susan Maidment (1984), *Child Custody and Divorce* (Beckenham, Croom Helm), pp. 147–8. This is not to claim that work or household financial management are equally shared during marriage. There is good evidence that they are not: see Stephen Edgell (1980), *Middle Class Couples* (London, George Allen and Unwin); Jan Pahl (1980), 'Patterns of Money Management within Marriage', 9 *Journal of Social Policy*, 313–37.

82. J. E. Todd and L. M. Jones (1972), *Matrimonial Property* (London, HMSO); Alberta Institute for Law Research and Reform (1974), *Matrimonial Property, Working Paper*; A. J. Manners and I. Rauta (1981), *Family Property in Scotland* (London, HMSO).

83. Gray (1977), ch. 4; Scot. Law Com. No. 67, paras. 369–77.

84. Manners and Rauta (1981), p. 16.

85. Lenore J. Weitzman (1981), 'The Economics and Divorce: Social and Economic Consequences of Property, Alimony and Child Support Awards', 28 *UCLA Law Rev.*, 1181–268.

86. See below, pp. 86–7.

87. For a comparison between the English and Californian practice in this regard, see Lenore J. Weitzman (1984), 'Divorce Outcomes in the United States and England: A Comparative Analysis of Property and Maintenance Awards', in John M. Eekelaar and Sanford N. Katz (eds.), *The Resolution of Family Conflict, Comparative Legal Perspectives* (Toronto, Butterworths), ch. 29. The importance of housing in the post-divorce lives of children is discussed below, pp. 73–9.

88. Per Lord Scarman in *Minton* v. *Minton* [1979] AC 593, at p.608.

89. Law Com. No. 103, para. 26.

90. *Dipper* v. *Dipper* [1981] Fam. 31; *Griffiths* v. *Griffiths* [1984] 3 WLR 165, per Watkins LJ.

91. Law Com. No. 103, para. 80.

92. Law Com. No. 112, para. 25.

93. For New Zealand, see W. R. Atkin (1981), 'Liable Relatives: The New State Role in Ordering Maintenance', 5 *Otago Law Rev.*, 48; European systems are described in Peter Dopfel and Bernd Buchhofer (1983), *Unterhaltsrecht in Europa* (Tübingen, J. C. B. Mohr). American developments are discussed in papers presented to the International Workshop on Child Support, directed by Alfred J. Kahn and Sheila B. Kamerman, Cross-National Studies, Columbia University (1985) (to be published).

94. Gray (1977), p. 320.

95. Law Com. No. 103, para. 85.

96. Scot. Law Com. No. 67, para. 3.95.
97. *Ibid.* para. 3.94.
98. See *McKay* v. *Essex Area Health Authority* [1982] 2 All ER 771.
99. Law Com. No. 112.
100. Law Com. No. 112, para. 24.
101. Ibid. paras. 26, 28, 39, and 42.
102. Matrimonial Proceedings Bill, Dec. 1981, presented by Mr Martin Stevens.
103. See Parliamentary Debates, *Special Standing Committee, Matrimonial and Family Proceedings Bill*, 20, 22 Mar. 1984.
104. Matrimonial Causes Act 1973, s. 25, as amended by the Matrimonial and Family Proceedings Act 1984, s. 3.
105. *Re B* [1976] Fam. 161 at p. 166, per Cumming-Bruce LJ; *re W* (*a minor: adoption*) (1984) 14 Family Law 179.
106. It is also possibly how the President of the Family Division understood its meaning: see Parliamentary Debates, *Special Standing Committee, Matrimonial and Family Proceedings Bill*, 22 Mar. 1984, cols. 76, 100.
107. See *Daubney* v. *Daubney* [1976] Fam. 267; *Furniss* v. *Furniss* (1982) 12 Family Law 30; *Stockford* v. *Stockford* (1982) 3 FLR 8; *Camm* v. *Camm* (1983) 13 Family Law 112; *Hall* v. *Hall* (1984) 14 Family Law 54.
108. Matrimonial Causes Act 1973, s. 25 (2) (a) as amended by the Matrimonial and Family Proceedings Act 1984, s. 3.
109. Matrimonial Causes Act 1973, ss. 25A (2), 31 (7) (a) as inserted by the Matrimonial and Family Proceedings Act 1984, ss. 3, 6.
110. Parliamentary Debates, ibid. col. 95.
111. *Dipper* v. *Dipper* [1981] Fam. 31; *Minton* v. *Minton* [1979] AC 593.
112. Matrimonial Causes Act 1973, s. 25A (3), as inserted by the Matrimonial and Family Proceedings Act 1984, s. 3.
113. Law Commission (1981), *Family Law: The Financial Consequences of Divorce*, Law Com. No. 112, para. 8.
114. Working Paper No. 12 (1975).
115. See *Report on Family Law, Part VI, Support Obligations* (1975).
116. *Seventh Report of the Royal Commission on Family and Children's, Law, Family Maintenance* (June 1975), p. 22.
117. Samuel F. Hofstadter and Shirley R. Levittan (1967), 'Alimony — A Reformulation', 7 *Journal of Family Law*, 51.
118. See Lenore J. Weitzman and Ruth Dixon (1980), 'The Alimony Myth: Does No-Fault Divorce Make a Difference?', 14 *Family Law Quarterly*, 141; Lenore J. Weitzman (1981), 'The Economics of Divorce: Social and Economic Consequences of Property, Alimony and Child Support Awards', 28 *UCCLA Law Rev.* 1181; Lenore J. Weitzman (1985) *The Divorce Revolution: The Unexpected Social and Economic Consequences for Women and Children in America* (New York, The Free Press/Macmillan.) A. Sorensen and M. MacDonald (1982), 'Does Child Support Support the Children?', 4 *Children and Youth Services Rev.* 53; David Chambers (1979), *Making Fathers Pay: The Enforcement of Child Support* (Chicago, University of Chicago Press).
119. B. Doig (1982), *The Nature and Scale of Aliment and Financial Provision on Divorce in Scotland* (Edinburgh Central Research Unit, Scottish Office).

4. The Nature and Purpose of the Study

As matters stood when the Law Commission issued its Discussion Paper in October 1980, information in the United Kingdom on the economic consequences of divorce was scant. Demographic data provided a reasonably clear picture of the social and economic characteristics of the divorcing population.[1] A variety of sources provided information about family incomes, the employment of women and groups in poverty generally.[2] Judicial statistics published annually described the legal process, but could not throw light on the impact of divorce on the people involved.[3] Small studies had begun to produce some evidence of the kinds of orders made by magistrates' courts and the higher courts.[4] But there had been no systematic attempt to draw this data together. Even if this task had been attempted it would have been difficult on the basis of existing data sets to gather accurate information about the economic consequences of divorce for those involved in the long term. Ideally such information could be obtained through a cohort study, contacting a group of divorcing couples at the time of divorce and collecting information from them over a period of time. The major British cohort studies of children born in 1946 and 1958[5] might appear useful sources in this respect. Indeed, as we report in Chapter 5, the 1946 cohort has provided some useful data. But the information concerning health and development which these studies has been designed to produce is not always relevant for our purpose, and the economic questions with which we are concerned are not fully covered.

We considered attempting to create our own cohort of divorcing couples through contacts made in selected divorce courts. However, we rejected this approach on a number of grounds. We were unsure how succesful we could be in maintaining contact with a group of people who were likely to be highly mobile, and, in the case of the women, subject to changes of name as well as address. But the major drawback was the length of time which must elapse before a cohort study can yield results. We felt the pressure of events. The campaign for reform of the law of maintenance was bearing political fruit. Debate in the media was insistent. We needed to produce the most reliable information obtainable as quickly as we could. Therefore, with the resources of the

ESRC Centre for Socio-Legal Studies, and additional support from the Equal Opportunities Commission, we were able to undertake our own small but nationally based survey of divorced men and women.

A screening question was asked on our behalf by an omnibus survey organization in May 1971 in the course of their interviews with a national quota sample of 8,000 adults matched with the general population by age, sex and socio-economic group, based on 200 sampling points throughout the United Kingdom. We were fortunate that the organization was willing to ask all its contacts whether they had been divorced since 1971 (when the new divorce law came into operation), if they were willing to accept interview on the financial matters pertaining to it and, if they were, to supply us with those names and addresses. In the event, of 7,257 adults screened in England and Wales, 718 reported members of their household had divorced within this period. Of these, 344 were unwilling to be reinterviewed. The comparatively low level of agreement to recall interview after this kind of initial contact has been documented in previous research.[6] But we had the advantage that in this case the original screening interviews had provided basic demographic data which enabled us to compare the demographic characteristics of those who accepted further interview and those who did not. There was very little difference between the two groups (see Table 4.1). We were therefore assured that our eventual sample suffered no undue bias on this account. The divorce reporters expressing willingness to be interviewed resided at 314 addresses. Ten were used in a pilot study refining the questionnaire, and twenty-three proved to be out of scope (either the divorce had not been finalized, or the addresses were vacant or derelict by the time of recall). At the 271 in-scope addresses, a final response rate of 85 per cent was achieved, yielding information on 92 men and 184 women in interviews carried out in November 1981. Although we were satisfied that our final sample was not unduly biased on demographic grounds, we needed to establish that it was also representative as regards divorce-related matters. We therefore checked, for example, the sex ratio of the petitioners and numbers of defended petitions against the national statistics, and found a close match. *Judicial Statistics* (HMSO, 1982) reported that in 1981, 74 per cent of petitioners were women, and in our sample 77 per cent of the women had petitioned. In 1981 nine out of ten of all divorces were granted under the special procedure used for undefended divorces, and only 9 per cent of our respondents reported contesting the divorce.

The proportion of men in our sample fell from 47 per cent of the

Table 4.1. *The demographic characteristics of the quota sample, the individuals reporting divorce, and those refusing recall*

	Total quota sample (n = 7,257) %	Divorce reporters (n = 718) %	Recall refusers (n = 344)† %
Male	47	43 (n = 319)	46 (n = 162)
Female	53	56 (n = 399)	55 (n = 182)
Age:			
16–24	12	16	18
25–34	23	27	26
35–54	32	39	35
54 and over	33	18	22
Women working	51	50	49
Children under 16 in household	49	56	52
Social grade:			
AB*	17	13	14
C1	22	21	20
C2	35	35	44
DE	27	32	27
Housing:			
Owner-occupied	59	45	51
Local authority rented	35	47	45
Other	5	7	5

* These grades use JICNARS definitions: A = higher managerial professional, or administrative; B = intermediate managerial, professional, or administrative; C1 = supervisory or clerical and junior managerial, professional, or administrative; C2 = skilled manual; D = semi- and unskilled manual; E = those at subsistence level, state pensions, and casual workers.
† Eight men and eleven women, unsure about recall, were therefore excluded.

screened out population to 43 per cent of the divorce reporters, 46 per cent of the interview refusers, and finally, to 33 per cent of the achieved sample. They disappeared gradually, as they tend to do in survey work, so we do not attribute the loss to a specific cause. In case the non productive addresses contained a disproportionate number of non-remarried mobile men, the screening interview data were checked for present marital status, and the ratio between remarried men and women in such addresses was found to be consistent with national statistics in showing that 44 per cent of the men were remarried as against 33 per cent of the women.[7] Our sample of divorced men also indicated an unemployment rate higher than the national average, but this is consistent with other data showing above average rates of unemployment among divorced men.[8] Finally, confidence in the representative nature of our final sample was strengthened by the close correspondence of our findings on specific issues with other research reported elsewhere, to which reference will be made in the course of the exposition of our findings.[9]

Our final sample of 276 individuals is, of course, relatively small. It was, however, central to our strategy that it should be as closely representative of the divorcing population at large as we could make it. We therefore chose not to distort our original sample by interviewing additional cases with particular characteristics. As a result some tables include cells based on small numbers of cases, which must be used with caution in attempting to formulate an overall picture. During the course of the analysis we became particularly interested in the circumstances of women with older children whose position in the labour market had been significantly affected by the responsibilities of child-rearing, but who were reaching the stage of no longer being entitled to support in their capacity as mothers of dependent children. As the number of such women in the 1981 survey was inevitably small, we did not increase numbers from convenient sources but decided to undertake a second survey in 1984 to obtain a larger but still representative sample of this category and elicit more precise information relevant to their circumstances. With the support of the Nuffield Foundation we approached the omnibus quota sample of 2,000 adults interviewed in March 1984, and screened out and successfully reinterviewed twenty-two women in this category of older mothers.

The Structure of the Analysis

Existing research on the economic consequences of divorce and indeed the debate surrounding the passage of the Matrimonial and Family Proceedings Act 1984, has tended to consider the economic impact of divorce in terms of its different effects for men and women. But as we examined our data, we concluded that a more illuminating approach could be achieved by considering the household as an economic unit containing economically productive and economically dependent members. Within each household there is a dependency ratio, which alters gradually over the life cycle of the family as members enter and leave the labour market according to their age, health, and child care responsibilities. But when a family is broken by divorce, the dependency ratio can alter immediately and fundamentally. We suggest that there are two distinct classes of divorced person and indeed of divorce process. Our data indicate that significant differences exist between divorces of childless marriages, where no dependency has been created, and marriages into which children have been introduced, creating economic dependency both directly and indirectly through their impact on the wife's earning capacity during and after the child rearing period. The change in the dependency ratio caused by the divorce may subsequently be further affected by cohabitation or remarriage, with the addition of a potential second income or the addition of new dependents for those who remarry a partner with existing children, or who go on to produce subsequent children. In the exposition of our data, therefore, we have constructed two categories of divorce: childless divorces and children divorces. We include in the former category all cases in which no child was introduced into the marriage. We include in the latter all cases where a child was introduced into the marriage, but this category is subdivided into those divorces where the children of the family had reached economic independence before the marriage ended, those where the children were dependent at the time of separation but have since become independent, and those where the children were still dependent. (See Table 4.2). As we went on to examine more closely the economic circumstances of families with children after divorce it became necessary to modify the original classification and define the families according to their current position. To the original children divorces we added families where children had been introduced after divorce by remarriage or cohabitation and excluded families where the youngest child had reached independence by the time of interview, thus forming the category of *families with dependent children*. For this part of the analysis we consider the 150 families which included a child aged under eighteen at the time of interview. Of these, fifty-two were headed by single parents, and ninety-eight contained two adults who had remarried or were cohabiting. Of the reconstituted group, thirty-six had only children from the first marriage, thirty-four had children from first and second marriages, and twenty-eight had children only from the second marriage. The initial analysis of this data was published as *Children and Divorce: Economic Factors.*[10]

Finally, a third categorization was developed to enable us to address the question of the economic circumstances of older women with older children of the marriage. For this purpose we have used the additional

Table 4.2. *Childless and children divorces (1981 sample)*

	Total	Reported by men	Reported by women
Childless divorces	46	20	26
Children divorces	183	48	135
Children adult (17+) at separation		3	4
Youngest child adult (17+) at time of interviews		10	27
At least one child under 17 in household at time of interview		35	104
Total	229	68	161

Note: All economic analysis reports household data. Where we interviewed more than one respondent per household the report given by the first contacted respondent is used. (Information from second respondents is used only in the legal analysis.)

data collected in 1984 to enable us to examine the situation of *long term mothers*, being women whose children have reached, or are approaching, independence. This group provides the data required for consideration of the long-term economic impact of child-rearing for non-remarried divorced woman as opposed to those with current entitlement to income support as caregiving mothers. Of this group of twenty-two women, 75 per cent were over forty, 77 per cent had been married for over ten years, half had no children still under sixteen, and half had children between twelve and sixteen as well as children over sixteen.

In addition, at some points in the analysis new subgroups are selected for specific purposes. For example, consideration of the resources of those paying maintenance required examination of a subgroup of those with children both in their present household and in other households, compared with those with children in other households but none in their present household. In some cases, as in the above, these categories overlap with those used in the basic structure. In each case the categories are clearly defined both in the text and in the tables.

The proportion of 'childless' to 'children' divorces in our sample is considerably lower than the proportion of divorces treated as 'childless' to 'children' divorces in the national statistics, which during the 1970s, was at a ratio of around 4 : 6.[11] However, as we have seen, our definition of 'childless' is narrower than in the national data, which defined childless divorces as those where there were no dependent children of the marriage at the time of filing the petition, but they could include instances where the divorce took place after the children were adult. Furthermore, 'dependent' is defined in the national statistics as being under sixteen. Many cases treated as 'childless' by those criteria would in fact fall within our category of 'children' divorces. We include children who are over sixteen but under eighteen in our definition of children because a child support order on divorce may extend up to eighteen (or beyond, if the child is in receipt of full-time education).[12] Furthermore, we have taken the time of separation rather than filing the divorce petition as the reference point for determining the presence of children. In 1971 Chester[13] calculated the median interval from separation to 'final divorce'[14] to be 2.9 years. Even taking into account the changes in substantive and procedural law since Chester's findings, it seems possible that many cases where the youngest child is only fourteen or fifteen at separation will appear as 'childless' by the official definitions although we of course treat them as 'children' divorces. It seems right to choose the presence of dependent children at the time of separation as the proper point in determining whether the divorce concerns children or not, for at that moment some arrangements for their support need to be (and often are) made. It also seems unrealistic, especially at a time of high levels of teenage unemployment, to assume that dependency ceases at sixteen. We suspect that the 4 : 6 ratio under-represents the proportion of divorces where problems relating to child support in fact arise. We estimate that if we had used the *official* definition, our 'childless' cases would constitute 33 per cent of our sample.[15] The two chapters which follow are concerned firstly with the economic consequences of divorce, and secondly with an examination of the various resources available to those affected.

Notes

1. Colin Gibson (1974), 'The Association betweeen Divorce and Social Class in England and Wales', 25 *British Journal of Sociology*, 79; Richard Leete (1979), *Changing Patterns of Family Formation and Dissolution in England and Wales 1964–76* (Office of Population and Censuses Surveys, London, HMSO); Barbara Thornes and Jean Collard (1979), *Who Divorces?* (London, Routledge).

2. *Family Expenditure Survey 1980* (1981) (London, HMSO); R. Layard (1978), *The Causes of Poverty, Royal Commission on the Distribution of Income and Wealth* Background Paper No.6, (London, HMSO); *Report of the Committee on One-Parent Families* (Finer Committee) (1974), Cmnd. 5629 (London, HMSO).

3. *Judicial Statistics, Annual Report* (1982) (London, HMSO).

4. O. R. McGregor, L. Blom-Cooper, and C. Gibson (1976), *Separated Spouses* (London,

Duckworth); W. Barrington Baker *et al.* (1977), *The Matrimonial Jurisdiction of Registrars* (Oxford, SSRC Centre for Socio-Legal Studies).

5. E. Atkins, N. M. Cherry, J. W. B. Douglas, E. Kiernard, and M. E. J. Wadsworth (1981), 'The 1946 British Birth Cohort Study: an account of the origins, progress and results of the National Survey of Health and Development', in S. A. Mednick and A. E. Baird (eds.), *An Empirical Basis for Primary Prevention* (Oxford, Oxford University Press); M. Kellmer Pringle (ed.) (1980), *The Needs of Children* (London, Hutchinson).

6. M. Maclean and H. Genn (1979), *Methodological Issues in Social Surveys* (London, Macmillan).

7. R. Leete and S. Anthony (1979), 'Divorce and Remarriage: A Record Linkage Study', *Population Trends*, No. 16 (London, HMSO), found that 55 per cent of men and 48 per cent of women who divorced in 1973 had remarried four and a half years later.

8. W. Daniel (1981), *The Unemployed Flow* (London, Policy Studies Institute): *General Household Survey, 1982* (1984, London, HMSO), Table 6.8, p. 107.

9. See especially pp. 70–1, 89, 92, 93.

10. Mavis Maclean and John Eekelaar (1983), *Children and Divorce: Economic Factors* (Oxford, ESRC Centre for Socio-Legal Studies).

11. John Haskey (1983), 'Children of Divorcing Couples', *Population Trends*, No. 31 (London, HMSO); Law Commission (1980), *Family Law: The Financial Consequences of Divorce: The Basic Policy*, Law Com. No. 103, p. 3.

12. Matrimonial Causes Act 1973, s. 29.

13. Robert Chester (1971), 'The Duration of Marriage to Divorce', 22 *British Journal of Sociology*, 172.

14. This seems to be taken as the time of decree nisi rather than decree absolute. He found the median interval from filing the 'petition to granting of the decree' to be less than seven months. It is almost certainly less under the reformed procedure.

15. There might have been some under-reporting of divorces involving short, childless marriages which took place many years before our screening interviews.

5. The Economic Consequences Following Divorce

We begin this chapter by comparing the economic circumstances of men and women divorced after childless marriages, with those of divorcees into whose marriages children had been introduced. Having detected a general movement into poverty by those with children, we examine in more detail the present economic position of all the households in our sample. This is determined largely by the dependency ratio, which reflects the relationship between the number of dependent children and of economically active family members contributing to their support. We therefore need to introduce a further subdivision, breaking down the children and childless divorces into two groups: those which have reconstituted a new two adult family through remarriage or cohabitation and those which have not. We conclude the chapter by drawing on data found in the 1946 birth cohort study to provide some evidence as to whether the experience of their parents' divorce has economic implications for children in the long term.

In order to make comparisons of income levels between these groups and also with the general population, we needed to be able to relate the total net disposable household income to a household equivalence scale, that is, a scale indicating the relationship between needs and means, which can provide a measure of a standard of living. The scales most widely understood in Britain for this purpose are those used by the supplementary benefit authorities.[1] We will return to these equivalence scales in our final evaluations in Chapters 7 and 8. In this context, we applied them by calculating the short term supplementary benefit entitlement (excluding allowances for special needs, but including the housing allowance) for each household at the time of the interview and, taking the mid-point in the band reported for total net disposable household income, we were able to calculate the income level of each family as a percentage of its supplementary benefit entitlement. This enabled us to compare our findings with the poverty studies which have used various cut-off points (such as 140 per cent or 120 per cent of supplementary benefit level) as measures of poverty.[2]

We also wished to place our groups in the context of some measure of average family income. This is a 'common-sense' concept which is extremely difficult to approach with precision. However, for our purposes it seemed reasonable to take the average income of a two-adult, two-child household as measured each year by the Family Expenditure Survey (FES) and to express this as a percentage of such a family's supplementary benefit entitlement, to enable us to compare our families with this constructed 'average' family. The average income of the FES two-adult, two-child family (assuming one child to be under ten and the other between ten and fifteen) amounted to 200 per cent of its supplementary benefit entitlement at November 1981 rates. We follow Layard[3] in using 140 per cent of supplementary benefit entitlement as our 'poverty line'.

Using this technique, Table 5.1 compares the net disposable household income of our sample of the divorced population with and without children of the marriage. Since 71 per cent of the general population have incomes above 140 per cent of supplementary benefit entitlement,[4] the table demonstrates that the childless divorcees closely resemble the general population, whereas those with children of the marriage fall well below the average. Of our 1984 sample of non-remarried mothers, only one in four was living above 140 per cent of supplementary benefit level and those whose children were all aged sixteen or over were worse off than those who still had younger children in the household.

Table 5.1. *Percentage of divorced men and women with present incomes above 140 per cent of supplementary benefit entitlement*

	Now alone	Now reconstituted	Total
I. *Childless divorces*			
Men	20% (n = 5)	80% (n = 15)	70%
Women	43% (n = 7)	74% (n = 19)	73%
II. *Children divorces*			
Men	39% (n = 18)	50% (n = 30)	46%
Women	11% (n = 64)	39% (n = 71)	36%

But there are important variations within these groups. The men of childless divorces who had not reconstituted a family tended to a standard well below the average. Since a man's personal income rarely changes on the event of his marriage (or remarriage) it seems likely that the explanation for the disparity between the men who remained alone and those who reconstituted is simply that men with very low incomes (due largely to unemployment or sickness) are far less likely to reconstitute. In the case of women, those of childless divorces who were still alone were worse off than the general population, but only because women as a whole generally are. Their wages are lower and their social security entitlements comprise the basic minimum welfare payments based on assessment of needs and means, rather than insurance benefits based at higher levels on a contribution record through employment.[5] Once they reconstituted, they fell into the standard pattern. Women living alone with children, however, fell very far below the average (only 18 per cent being above 140 per cent of supplementary benefit entitlement). Equally important, it appears that divorcees (whether men or women) with dependent children, unlike the childless, do not generally recover to the national average when they reconstitute with another partner. This is because they tend to be a little older, and to have larger families, introducing children from previous partnerships and producing more.[6]

In view of the evidence[7] of the prevalence of divorce among lower-income groups, it may be thought that these data simply reflect the lower than average living standards of the divorcing population rather than the effects of divorce itself. But the difference between the categories of divorcing individuals makes this unlikely. The presence of children is clearly of decisive importance in determining the post-divorce standard of living of both male and female divorcees. It would appear that the economic effects of divorce itself have a significant impact on this group. We can demonstrate this in another way by viewing the economic circumstances of the families with children, over time. In a retrospective study, such as ours, the best measure of economic well-being over time, avoiding difficulties and adjustments for inflation when dealing with actual amounts of money, is to look at an individual's or a family's, main source of income. When a welfare payment is described as the chief source of income, as we can assume that the family is living, at best, at the margin of poverty. The results, for our sample of families with children, are shown in Table 5.2.

Reconstitution can be seen to have played an important part in determining whether reliance on welfare payments continued. Of the fifty-two parents with children under eighteen at separation, who remained sole parents at the time of interview, 56 per cent were mainly reliant on supplementary benefit when interviewed. Their position had worsened since divorce (when 46 per cent of these parents had been in that position). On the other hand, only 15 per cent of parents who had reconstituted a family which included children, whether the children derived from the first family, the second, or both, were mainly dependent

Table 5.2. *Divorced parents reporting welfare payments as their main source of income, over time*

Present status of respondent	At marriage	At separation	At divorce	November 1981
Single parents (n = 52)	0	8 (15%)	24 (46%)	29 (56%)
Reconstituted parents with children from first marriage (n = 36)	1	3	10	7
Reconstituted parents with children from first and second marriages (n = 34)	0	0	4	3
Reconstituted parents with children from second marriage (n = 28)	0	5	3	4
		} 8%	} 17%	} 15%
Total	1	16 (11%)	41 (27%)	45 (29%)

on welfare payments when interviewed. Both categories, however, were much worse off than they had been at the time of their first marriage.

Other studies have produced very similar results. In Britain, data on women caring for dependent children interviewed three months after divorce showed that while only 2 per cent were in receipt of social security payments prior to separation, this had risen to one-third at the time of the interview.[8] The longitudinal study data provided by the American Panel Study of Income Dynamics, analysed by Hoffman (1977), showed that between 1967 and 1973, the real income of families unaffected by separation or divorce rose by 21.7 per cent whereas that of women who divorced or separated during that period fell by 29.3 per cent. Relating income to needs (by relating the Department of Agriculture's Low Cost Food Budget to the size and the age/sex composition of the family) the standard of living of the intact family rose by 20.8 per cent and that of divorced or separated women fell by 6.7 per cent.[9] Since it is overwhelmingly likely that children will be associated with the woman after divorce,[10] this decline in living standards relative to the intact family will usually be suffered by the individual left with the dependent children of the marriage.

This type of information supplements the well-documented evidence of the relative poverty of one-parent families in Western societies. We do not intend to review this evidence here.[11] What our data can enable us to do is to *compare* the economic circumstances of those individuals forming a one-parent family after divorce, with the circumstances of other individuals who have experienced divorce but do not constitute a one-parent family, either because they live alone without children in the household or because they have formed a new two-parent household. Tables 5.3, 5.4, and 5.5 compare those divorcees who were still living in a single parent family household at time of interview (n = 52), with those who had 'reconstituted' (n = 98), and those parents who had neither custody of the child of the marriage nor any other child (n = 19). Table 5.3 shows their actual incomes; Table 5.4 shows that nearly two-thirds of the lone parents were living close to or below the supplementary benefit level, and that four out of five (79 per cent) were below our poverty line of 140 per cent of supplementary benefit entitlement, whereas less than one-fifth of reconstituted families were close to, or below, supplementary benefit

Table 5.3. *Household income (total net weekly disposable) of single, reconstituted, and non-caregiving parents*

	Single parents (n = 52)	Reconstituted parents (n = 98)	Non-caregiving parents without children in household now (n = 19)
£			
to 30	0	1	1
30–59	17	4	2
60–89	26	19	6
90–119	4	20	1
120–49	2	21	3
150–79	2	10	2
180–209	1	11	3
210 +	0	8	0
Don't Know	0	4*	1

* Three cohabiting women could not report total household income.

Table 5.4. *Household net disposable income as percentage of supplementary benefit entitlement for each family, for single, reconstituted, and non-caregiving parents*

% Supplementary benefit	Single (n = 52) %	Reconstituted (n = 98) %	Non-caregiving parent without children in household (n = 19)
300 +	4	9	20
250–299	2	5	25
200–49	2	12	0
'happy family' line			
180–99	0	8	10
160–79	2	9	0
140–59	10	20	5
poverty line			
110–39	17	13	25
90–109	31	11	5
Below 90	31	6	10
Don't Know	2	5	0

Table 5.5. *Average disposable household incomes of single and reconstituted parents, in quantiles, presented as a percentage of supplementary benefit entitlements*

	Single parent (n = 52) % SBE	Reconstituted households (n = 98) % SBE	2-adult, 2-child FES family* (n = 1046) % SBE
Top decile	268	327	328
Top quantile	185	279	254
Median	96	158	200
Lowest quantile	72	102	150
Lowest decile	67	84	112

* See FES 1982, Table 26, p. 72.

level, and one-third were below the poverty level. Fewer than one in ten of our single parent families enjoyed what could be called an 'average family' standard of living, compared with one in four of the reconstituted families. The non-caregiving parents without children in their present household were less likely to appear in the just-above-poverty/just-under-average group than those from the reconstituted families, but more likely to appear at both extremes.

To give a clearer picture of the spread of the income distributions of these households in relation to those of the average (FES) family, we divided our single and reconstituted parents into quantiles in order to compare our data with the FES data for 1981.[12] Table 5.5 makes it possible for us to see the size of the gap between the standard of living of single and reconstituted parents, and also the nature of the gap between the standard of living of reconstituted parents and the average two-adult, two-child household. Although the incomes of the top quantile of reconstituted parents is very close to that of the FES family, the median income and the lower quantile of the reconstituted family are clearly below that of the 'average' family. Although their earning capacity is not affected by divorce and remarriage, yet their overall standard of living probably reflects the prevalence of divorce amongst lower income households and the larger family size which may result from a remarrying woman bringing with her children from a former marriage and going on to have more.

Thus far our data demonstrate the exceptional adversity relative both to other groups of divorced individuals and to the population at large suffered by single parents in terms of income. Reference should also be made to the housing situation of these individuals. A move from the owner-occupier sector to the private renter sector, or from the private to public sector, may have a significant impact on an existing standard of living.[13]

A distinction needs to be drawn between occupants of local authority housing at the time of separation and those enjoying other types of housing provision. In the former case, the childless invariably left the accommodation. But where there were children, 79 per cent of the women interview respondents (n = 52) and 30 per cent of the men (n = 21) stayed; all but one of the men having custody of the children (see Tables 5.6 and 5.7). Of the few women who left, three returned (with their children) to their own families, four moved into a house with their new partners, and in one case both parents left and were re-housed by the local authority. For these people, then, housing circumstances in themselves played no significant role in altering their living standards on divorce. The effects of divorce would primarily be felt in respect to income. A similar pattern was found among the long-term mothers interviewed in 1984. Eight out of the ten in local authority housing at separation stayed there, the other two moving into owner-occupation (one with married children and one buying her council house).

Table 5.6. *Housing position of owner-occupiers on divorce: childless divorces*

	Total		House sold		Husband stayed		Wife stayed		Husband left with share		Wife left with share		Husband left without share		Wife left without share	
	Col. No. %		Row %	No.	Row %	No.	Row %	No.	Row %	No.	Row %	No.	Row %	No.	Row %	No.
House in joint names	81	22	50	11	45	10*	4	1	50	11	77	17	0	0	13	3
House in husband's name	19	5	20	1	80	4	0	0	20	1	20	1	0	0	80	4
Total	100	27	44	12	52	14	3	1	44	12	66	18	0	0	26	7

* This may be an underestimate; more women reporters said the house was sold than men reporters. The latter reported a higher rate of men staying. It is possible the women assumed the house was sold (for they received a lump sum) whereas in fact the men stayed on.

Table 5.7. *Housing position of owner-occupiers on divorce: children divorces*

	Total		House sold		Husband stayed		Wife stayed		Husband left with share		Wife left with share		Husband left without share		Wife left without share	
	Col. %	No.	Row %	No.	Row %	No.	Row %	No.	Row %	No.	Row %	No.	Row %	No.	Row %	No.
House in joint names	72	48	52	25†‡	25	12‡	23	11ξ	38	27‡	62	30	10	7¶	10	5¶
House in husband's name	18	12	33	4‖	33	4	25	3	17	3	33	4	17	3	25	3
House in wife's name	6	4	50	2	0	0	50	2	33	2	50	2	33	2	0	0
Don't know	4	2	0	0	0	0	50	1**	0	0	0	0	25	1**	0	0
Total	100	66	46	31	24	16	26	17	88	32	54	36	8¶	13	12	8

† Includes two cases of foreclosure.
‡ Includes one custodial father.
ξ Includes three 'Mesher' arrangements (one by court order).
¶ Includes one case where husband kept custody of one child and one where a non-custodial mother left his share 'on trust' for the children.
‖ Includes one foreclosure.
** This was a 'Mesher' order.

But when we look at the housing outcome with respect to the owner-occupiers, a more complex picture emerges. Tables 5.6 and 5.7 show that childless and children divorces share one feature regarding the home. In almost half of each category, the owner-occupied home was sold on divorce. In the case of the childless, the reason for the sale seems to have been to allow the wife to realize her half-share in the house, for half the homes of such couples which were in their joint names were sold. If the house was not sold, it was much more likely that the husband would stay on in the home than the wife, but in that event the wife would invariably leave with a lump sum payment; the husband had bought her out. In the three cases (13 per cent) where the wife left without a share, she went straight into a home provided by another man. If the house was in the husband's name alone, he was overwhelmingly likely to remain in it and the wife to leave without any lump sum payment. It is possible that in some of those cases the wife went uncompensated for any beneficial interest she may have acquired in the home by reason of direct or indirect monetary contributions to its acquisition.[14] The advantage, from a wife's point of view, of joint legal ownership is clear, and the message of these findings seems to be that, for childless marriages, a lump sum payment made to the wife is likely to be in the form of strict compensation for the transfer to the husband of a property interest.

It is striking that owner-occupied homes are just as likely to be sold in the case of divorces involving dependent children as where the marriage was childless, despite the well-established policy of the courts that one of the primary goals of divorce settlement is to secure accommodation for the children, usually by keeping them in the matrimonial home. Are the children of divorcees who live in the owner-occupier sector subject to greater disruption than those of divorcees who live in public-sector housing?

In a number of cases it might be unnecessary to keep the home for the children because they and the wife will be moving into accommodation provided by another man. In four (28 per cent) of the cases where the house was sold the woman moved in with a new partner. So in over a quarter of the cases where the home was sold, no accommodation problem for the children arose. What of the other cases? It seems that the sales in these cases might either have been desired by the caregiving parent wanting to move from the area, or forced on her by the financial situation. This can be deduced from the fact that the wife stayed on in the house only once (3 per cent) in the childless cases, but did so in *one-quarter* of the children cases, irrespective of whether the house was in joint names or in the husband's name alone. Put another way, the wife stayed in half of the cases where the home was not sold. The reason for this is undoubtedly to provide accommodation for the children, and there is no reason to believe that this would not have happened in those cases where the house was sold were it not for the fact that the wife desired the sale or had it forced on her. Indeed, a small number of the sales (10 per cent) were in fact the result of foreclosure by the mortgagee. Others may well have taken place to prevent this eventuality.

It is at this point, of course, that the difficulties which the families with children experience over income have direct impact on their housing conditions. Yet, about three-quarters of the divorced mothers, still single and with dependent children, who had been in owner-occupation at the time of their separation were still living in *the private sector* at the time of interview. The lump sum acquired by the sale, or support from the former husband, or payments of mortgage interest by the supplementary benefit authorities, cushioned the *extent* of the deterioration in their housing circumstances; or, at least, the degree to which they needed to go to the public housing authorities for assistance. It is plausible to suppose that a move from the private sector will frequently cause greater social disruption, especially as regards the children's school environment, than moves within a sector. Our data showed that, of the women who moved, half (seven) were able to buy in the private sector (three of them later remarried). Only three (21 per cent) moved into public housing.

Our findings regarding the housing circumstances of divorcing men fail to show any disturbing degrees of hardship. In the childless cases, the man either kept the house or sold it, taking his share. Even where there were children, he stayed on in the house in one-quarter of the cases. Where the wife stayed, we found no evidence that she was joined by a cohabitee or new husband. The pattern seems clearly to be that, where a new partner enters the scene, he will provide a home for the wife and children. Where, in the divorces involving dependent children, the home was sold, the husband invariably took his share. There were, however, a few cases (thirteen (22 per cent) of those where either the house was sold or the wife remained in it) where the husband left without any apparent immediate compensation for his capital loss. However, four involved a 'Mesher' arrangement whereby the house is settled on trust for sale for both parents but sale is postponed until the youngest child reaches a certain age (usually eighteen or on completion of full-time education), or until a court order is made.[15] Thus the husband is not deprived of his capital; his enjoyment of it is simply postponed. Of the seven cases where the husband left without taking any share of the asset, three forewent their share in discharge of their support obligation, one went to a new partner with a house and we had no information on the others. It should be remembered, of course, that when it is the man who leaves, it will usually be very difficult for the wife to raise sufficient capital to pay him a lump sum. Her inferior earning power and commitments to the children effectively preclude such a course.

The long-term mothers in owner-occupation at the time of separation were perhaps more firmly established in this sector. Even so, in half of the cases the home was sold and the proceeds shared enabled the women to buy a smaller property. Of the cases where the house was not sold, in half the house was occupied in lieu of maintenance (in one case with a 'Mesher' agreement), and in the two remaining cases the wife purchased her husband's interest, one with her own resources and the other with parental help.

We should conclude this review of the economic conditions of families after divorce by remarking on the significance of housing provision. Were it not for the relative security provided by public-sector housing, the position of many divorced single mothers would be far worse than it is. As we have seen, there is no potential in income transfers to substitute for its absence. We might make the same observation with respect to health care. It is fortunately not essential for these mothers to rely on income provision, from the state or from the absent parent, to meet the medical expenses of their children. These fall on the community through the national health service. But even outside the ambit of community-financed services, we note that, as far as accommodation is concerned, the position of mothers living in the private sector is not totally bleak. Most managed to stay in that sector, even if precariously. The attention given to the accommodation of children by judicial policy seems, according to our data, to have borne some fruit and, in so far as it has done so, has reduced the extent to which the receipt of income maintenance is critical to the most fundamental needs of these families. The Social Security Review of 1985 revealed that the government was concerned about the burden which housing-related benefit (whether by way of rate rebates, payment of rent and mortgage interest, and of water and heating charges) was placing on the social security budget (*Reform of Social Security* (1985) Cmnd. 9587). The implications of any erosion of these benefits for families broken by divorce do not seem to have been considered. The result might be to throw them into greater dependence on maintenance from the absent parent, to undermine the already precarious degree to which stability in housing those in owner-occupation has been achieved and to put new pressure on the public sector.

Longer-term Consequences

Of the longer-term consequences of the divorce of childless marriages, at least if it takes place relatively early in the marriage, we need feel no concern. There is nothing in our data to suggest that the fact of divorce has any significant economic impact on the partners' circumstances; nor is it plausible to suppose that it should. If it could be shown that women changed their employment pattern significantly simply on entering marriage (rather than on the expectation, and subsequent rearing, of children) it might be argued that the breakdown of the marriage may disadvantage such a woman when set alongside other women who have not borne children, and who have not married. Evidence is beginning to emerge on this point from a small cohort study which describes young brides changing their jobs to fit in with their new domestic duties at marriage rather than on the birth of their first child.[16] If this were so to any significant degree, there might be a case for considering compensation for such a loss (we discuss this in Chapter 8). But it seems that any changes made are of little consequence compared with changes related to child care responsibilities.

Our primary concern must be directed at the implications which the economic adversity afflicting one-parent families after divorce holds for the children and the adults in this group. The evidence we have reviewed earlier in this chapter shows the degree of that hardship and the scale on which it extends to single parent families. But it does not indicate for how long such conditions persist for these families. It is clear from our data that reconstitution into a two-adult family is the most significant means of at least partially recovering former economic status. But we have little information on the duration of single parenthood, which age-groups of children are likely to be affected, and for what periods of time. Leete and Anthony (1979) have shown that at four and a half years after divorce, nearly half of divorced women have remarried and that one-third of these did so within three months of divorce. They also found that the presence of children did not in itself seem to affect remarriage prospects. Age at divorce was a far more significant factor. The older the woman at divorce, the less was the likelihood of her remarrying. Where the youngest child was over ten at the time of the divorce, the chances of remarriage dropped.[17] It would seem, therefore, that reconstitution is more likely where the woman (and therefore the children) are younger. However, this evidence provides no information on the economic circumstances of the individuals concerned (are the poorer less or more likely to reconstitute than the better off, or is wealth irrelevant?). If families with older children are less likely to reconstitute, what is the relative impact of divorce on younger and older children? Our available evidence indicates a complex situation. The economic needs of older children are clearly greater and their decisions about further education and training may be affected with significant consequences for their future earning capacity. But although the younger children of younger mothers are more likely to improve their economic position through reconstitution nevertheless the adverse effects of life in a single parent family as measured by later medical and psychological criteria have been shown to be associated with separation occurring before the age of five.[18]

It appears, however, that there is no significant economic improvement over time for these households, either for the single mothers or the older mothers interviewed in 1984. The poverty which follows divorce appears to be a long-term problem and therefore any attempt at relief through a high-level crisis-oriented benefit, analogous to the short-term high rate of benefit paid to widows, would not be appropriate. Our data yield some information on the relationship between length of time spent in a one-parent family (over half our single mothers had been separated for more than five years) and the economic position of the family at the time of interview. We found no relationship between length of time since separation and the likelihood of reporting social security as the main source of household income. Exactly the same proportion of those separated for less than five years and for five years or more reported social security as their main source of income.

We cannot say for certain what will happen to these children in adult life. Although we do not have longitudinal data in the Oxford Survey, fortunately we are able to add to our data new material from the Medical Research Council National Survey of Health and Development, 1946 British birth cohort, concerning the long-term impact on children of parental divorce. Data from the study have been used to examine the educational achievements of adults who in childhood experienced parental divorce, comparing their achievements with those of other members of the cohort. This is the first time the longitudinal data has been examined in this way in the United Kingdom, and the results are disturbing.

The National Survey study population comprises all legitimate single births to wives of non-manual and agricultural workers, and one in four of legitimate single births to manual workers that occurred in the week 3–9 March 1946, comprising a total of 5,362 children. This cohort was studied at birth and at intervals of not more than two years throughout childhood and adolescence, and at approximately five year intervals in adult life so far up to the age of thirty-six years. Work specifically concerned with the incidence and later effects of divorce and separation has until now concentrated on medical and behavioural aspects, and may be found in Rowntree (1955), Douglas (1970), and Wadsworth (1976, 1979, 1984).[19] Our analysis, however, is concerned to establish whether the breakup of a family through divorce or separation, rather than death, can be seen to affect the subsequent education and occupational attainment of the children. But it is worth noting that children from divorced or separated households were themselves significantly less likely to have married by the age of twenty-six years (Wadsworth 1984).

Table 5.8 shows that children from divorced or separated homes were significantly more likely than those from intact homes to have no educational qualifications by the age of twenty-six years, or to have a significantly reduced chance of acquiring qualifications at any level; and this association is maintained regardless of the social class of the family at the time of the breakup. In comparison, parental death – and these are mostly deaths of fathers (130 father deaths, 60 mother deaths) — seems to have very little impact on the child's later educational qualifications. This association of family circumstances with achieved level of education is statistically significant for both boys and girls.

Table 5.9. shows that, in contrast to our data showing that remarriage can substantially alleviate the economic reverses of divorce, it seems to do little to improve the educational prospects of the children involved. The numbers were too small for differentiation according to social class and this is a matter which requires further investigation.

We are not entirely sure whether these effects are a result of father absence *per se*, father absence resulting in mother absence at work, or simply the effect of lower incomes. But we note their consistency with McLanahan's (1985) conclusions from the American Panel Study of Income Dynamics which associated low school attendance at seventeen and poor high school graduation of children of mother-only families with economic deprivation rather than parental absence. Furthermore,

Table 5.8. *Changes in circumstances of families from different social classes and their association with the child's later educational achievement.*

Family circumstances	Child's achieved level of education by age 26 years				Total (= 100 %)
	Number of qualifications	Up to and including 'O' level	'A' level and equivalents	University	
I. *Non-manual classes:*					
Not broken	16.9	28.7	35.2	19.2	1,471
Broken by divorce or separation	42.9	20.4	25.5	11.2	98
Broken by death of a parent	22.0	34.9	33.0	10.1	109
II. *Manual social classes*					
Not broken	53.2	27.6	16.6	2.6	1,936
Broken by divorce or separation	67.9	24.2	7.3	0.6	165
Broken by death of a parent	61.1	22.2	13.0	3.8	185

Non-manual social classes x^2 = 47.29 with 6 d.f. (p. <001).
Manual social classes x^2 = 20.61 with 4 d.f. (adding cols 3 and 4) (p. <001).

Table 5.9. *The associations of custodial parent's remarriage with the study child's later educational achievements*

Family circumstances whilst child aged 0–14 years	Child's achieved level of education by age 26 years				Total (= 100%)
	Number of qualifications	Up to and including 'O' level	'A' level and equivalents	University	(= 100%)
Not broken	37.15	26.1	24.7	9.7	3,407
Broken by divorce*					
Not remarried	58.4	19.5	15.9	6.2	113
Remarried	56.7	26.7	12.2	4.4	90
Broken by death of a parent†					
Not remarried	52.1	36.8	9.2	1.8	163
Remarried	51.8	18.8	22.3	7.1	85

* $x^2 = 1.94$ with 3 d.f. Not significant.
** $x^2 = 17.14$ with 3 d.f. p < .001

such lack of educational attainment has been found to be a major predictor of subsequent poverty and welfare receipt.[20] But whatever the causal relationship, these findings confirm our picture of socio-economic disadvantage for children affected by divorce, stretching into the future, which is mitigated but not removed by remarriage.

Notes

1. R. van Slooten and A. G. Coverdale (1978). 'The characteristics of low income households', *Social Trends* (London, HMSO) No. 8, pp. 27–9. On the importance of using equivalence scales in considering horizontal equity between families, see Joseph J. Seneca and Michael K. Taussig (1971), 'Family Equivalence Scales and Personal Income Tax Exemptions for Children', 53 *Rev. of Economics and Statistics*, 253–62; Samuel A. Rea (1984), 'Taxes, Transfers and the Family', 34 *Univ. of Toronto Law Journal*, 314–40.

2. R. Layard (1978), *The Causes of Poverty, Royal Commission on the Distribution of Income and Wealth*, Background Paper No. 6 (London, HMSO).

3. Ibid.

4. *Social Trends* No. 12 (1982) (London, HMSO), p. 72 (referring to 1980 data).

5. H. Land (1983), 'Poverty and Gender', in M. Brown (ed.), *The Structure of Disadvantage* (London, Heinemann).

6. Myra Wolfe, personal communication, 1983.

7. Graham B. Spanier and Paul C. Glick (1981), 'Marital instability in the United States: some correlates and recent changes', 30 *Family Relations*, 29; C. Gibson (1974), 'The Association between divorce and social class in England and Wales', 25 *British Journal of Sociology*, 79; Barbara Thornes and Jean Collard (1979), *Who Divorces?* (London, Routledge).

8. Gwyn Davis, Alison Macleod, and Mervyn Murch (1983), 'Divorce: Who Supports the Family?', 13 *Family Law*, 217: the sample was not a nationally representative one, and the slightly lower incidence of social-security reliance than in our sample may reflect the economic character of the region of the study.

9. Saul Hoffman (1977), 'Marital Instability and the Economic Status of Women', 14 *Demography*, 67.

10. In only 10 per cent of a national sample of divorce cases in 1974 were the children left with the father only: J. Eekelaar and E. Clive, with K. Clarke and S. Raikes, (1977), *Custody after Divorce* (Oxford, SSRC Centre for Socio-Legal Studies).

11. Reference may be made to the following literature: Finer Report (1974), vol. 11, paras. 5.19–20; Elsa Ferri (1976), *Growing-up in a One Parent Family* (London, National Council for Educational Research in England and Wales); Wilfred Beckerman and Stephen Clark (1982), *Poverty and Social Security in Britain since 1961* (Oxford, Oxford University Press); Jennie Popay, Lesley Rimmer, and Chris Rossiter (1983), *One Parent Families: Parents, Children and Public Policy* (London, Study Commission on the Family); Mary Ann Glendon (1981), *The New Family and the New Property* (Toronto, Butterworths), pp. 86, 134; *Poverty in Australia: Report of the Commission of Inquiry into Poverty in Australia* (1975) (Canberra, Australian Government Publishing Service).

12. *Family Expenditure Survey 1982* (London, HMSO).
13. A. Murie (1983), *Housing, Inequality and Deprivation* (London, Heinemann); S. Merrett and F. Gray (1982), *Owner Occupation in Britain* (London, Routledge and Kegan Paul).
14. See *Gissing* v. *Gissing* [1971] AC 886.
15. *Mesher* v. *Mesher* [1980] 1 All ER 126 n.
16. Penny Mansfield, The *Guardian*, 9 Feb. 1982.
17. Richard Leete and Susan Anthony (1979), 'Divorce and Remarriage: A Record Linkage Study', *Population Trends*, No. 16 (London, HMSO).
18. M. Wadsworth (1984), 'Early stress and associations with adult behaviour and parenting', in W. R. Butler and B. D. Corver (eds.), *Stress and Disability in Childhood* (Bristol, John Wright and Sons).
19. G. Rowntree (1955), 'Early Childhood in Broken Families', 8 *Population Studies*, p. 247; J. Douglas (1970), 'Broken Families and Child Behaviour', 4 *Journal of Royal College of Physicians*, pp. 203–10; M. E. J. Wadsworth (1979), 'Early life events and later behavioural outcomes', in S. B. Sells *et al.* (eds.), *Human Functioning in Longitudinal Perspective* (Baltimore, Williams and Wilkins).
20. Sara McLanahan (1985), 'Family Structure and the Reproduction of Poverty', 90 *American Journal of Sociology* 873.

6. The Resources Available After Divorce

On divorce there are essentially four sources from which economic support for the individuals affected by it may be drawn. The first comprises the resources of the former family as they stood at the moment of dissolution. The second and third are found in the earning capacity of each of the adults. The last resource is state provision. We must also remember the effects of reconstitution on the family dependency ratio, for, while we do not class this as a necessarily available resource, its occurrence introduces a powerful new factor bearing on the economic condition of the divorced family. The purpose of this chapter is to search our data to reveal the interplay between these elements, not only at the time of divorce, but also afterwards; for it is only in this way that the effects of legislative policies and judicial practices regarding post-divorce finances can be properly understood.

I. Resources of the Former Family

Apart from the home, fewer than one in five of the families in our total sample (n = 274) had savings of over £500 at the time of the divorce. Even surveys of currently married people[1] have indicated how little, apart from the home, most families accumulate by way of capital assets. The position is clearly rather worse for those who divorce. Where the divorce involves dependent children, it is worse still. As many as *one-third* of this group in our sample reported that their real problem was how to deal with debts, not assets. Where there were items of property, it proved harder for those with children to come to a satisfactory agreement about them than it was for the childless. Three-quarters of the latter reported a satisfactory arrangement, whereas just over one half of the former were satisfied. Rules about asset sharing on divorce, to which so much academic (and legislative) attention has been paid, though obviously necessary, will clearly have little relevance to the overall economic state of the post-divorce life of most people, especially those with children.

The extent to which the housing resources of the former family are re-distributed on divorce, was reviewed in the previous chapter. Where the original family lived in public-sector housing (where the house is not strictly speaking a resource), it was noted that the childless normally left the accommodation, whereas those with children stayed in it. If the home was owner-occupied, and registered in the joint names of the spouses, the childless, in equal proportions, either sold the house (sharing the proceeds) or permitted the former husband to remain living in it. If it was registered in the husband's name only, he stayed in it. Where there were children, the wife (caregiver) stayed on in a *quarter* of such cases, irrespective of the position regarding legal title. (See Table 5.7.) This does not indicate a particularly high degree of continued use for the caregiver and children of the family home. We suggested that a major reason for this could be the difficulty which such a caregiver would have in maintaining mortgage payments. Of the seventeen wives who stayed in the home, only four were able to take over responsibility for these payments. Two reported that their husbands had kept responsibility for them in lieu of making maintenance payments. Others were helped by the supplementary benefit authorities. Their position seems precarious and is likely to become more so if reductions in housing benefit predicted in 1985 come about. On the other hand, we also noted that three-quarters of divorced mothers, still single and with dependent children who had been in owner-occupation at the time of the divorce, were still living in the private sector at the time of interview. Two-thirds of the women who left the home took some share of the proceeds with them (we were unable to ascertain its precise extent) and this may have helped in keeping them in this sector. But their overall living standard reflected the combination of this element with the other resources which we will consider presently.

In housing, as in other matters, reconstitution becomes a most significant determinant of housing status. This is most clearly seen in the case of those families with dependent children who had reconstituted at time of interview (n = 98). Thirty-four of these had been in local authority housing at the time of the separation, and the majority remained there when they reconstituted, except for a group of eight (23 per cent) who moved into owner-occupied housing with their new partners. Twenty-three were renting in the private sector at time of separation, and half (all women) moved into owner-occupied housing on reconstitution. As remarked above, it was rare for a woman to stay on in owner-occupied housing unless she had children. Those who reconstituted stayed on even more rarely, despite the presence of children. This is because they tended to move to accommodation provided by the new partner. Twenty-four of the twenty-nine women in this category left the house, sixteen (two-thirds) going into owner-occupation provided in this way (nine of them taking some share from their original home). Only five women in this category stayed on in the matrimonial home (one bought out her husband; two held it on trust for sale with their former partner). The conclusion is that the housing resources of the first family are not generally being used as a foundation for the mother's second family. On reconstitution her housing status will depend primarily on her new partner, although in some cases she may be assisted by a small lump sum from the sale of the first house. The husband, on the other hand, is likely to stay in the former matrimonial home and use this as a base for his new family. Seven out of the twelve men (58 per cent) with dependent children who reconstituted did this, and of the five who left the house, two bought again as owner-occupiers, one went into local authority housing, one moved into his new partner's own home, and the fifth went into his new partner's local authority house. The men were more likely to use the housing resources of their first family towards their new family. Their earning power must be a significant factor in allowing them to do this. If we look at the housing status of all the parents who remarried, we find that this differs little from that of the population as a whole. Over half (53 per cent) achieve owner-occupation (the national figure is 55 per cent)[2] compared with less than one-third of the parents who remained single.

II. Present Sources of Income: Earnings, Maintenance, and Social Security

Maintenance payments essentially represent an assignment of part of the earning capacity of one individual in favour of the other. The maintenance recipient may supplement his or her earning capacity by this share in that of the former spouse. In an extreme case, the potential income which a recipient has the capacity to earn may be replaced by income derived from the maintenance payer. In this section we are primarily concerned with the interrelationship between these factors.

It is clear that maintenance is overwhelmingly paid by men to women. In our sample we had no instance of a woman paying maintenance to a caregiving father, although one such order existed but was not complied with. It is reasonable, for ease of analysis, to proceed on the assumption that it is the former wife who is the potential maintenance recipient. We first consider how far this position had any effect on her employment practice.

(a) Employment patterns

Of the women who had experienced childless divorces, half were working (15 per cent part time, 35 per cent full time) by the time we interviewed them. This group, however, includes both the older women who are less likely to remarry and who may be approaching retirement as well as younger women who have remarried and subsequently produced children. So few of this group received maintenance that we cannot discern any relationship between income from this source and propensity to work.

If we look at the single mothers with dependent children at the time of interview (n = 47), we find that 55 per cent were in employment, of whom one-third were working full time. The General Household Survey showed that 56 per cent of divorced lone mothers were employed, but nearly half of them worked full time.[3] These proportions are not very different from those relating to the economic activity of all women with dependent children, of whom 52 per cent are in paid work (one-third of them part time). Divorced single parents are slightly more likely to be in paid work than married women with dependent children (only 52 per cent) and to be working full time.[4] As these women grow older, a large proportion of them go out to work. Two-thirds of our long-term mothers were in employment, 52 per cent full time. The remainder had good reason not to work through sickness, disability, or retirement. Only one in ten thought of herself as a housewife. Martin's (1984) national study of women's employment describes how the proportion of women working increases with their age, and the age of their youngest child, up to fifty years, after which employment rates drop.

This pattern suggests that, as these women are gradually released from the responsibilities of child caregiving, they will seek employment in greater numbers than is usual for mothers who still have dependent children. Yet, as we saw in the previous chapter, the overall economic position of these women was particularly poor. This may not be, as Davis *et al.* (1983)[5] suggested, so much because the inducements of low-paid work are insufficient to draw them off dependence on social security (the so-called 'poverty trap') but because of their commitment to child caregiving. When they are free to work, they seek it. This was so even though many of our long-term mothers reported having taken jobs well below their former levels of skill and experience owing to the difficulty of reintroduction into the labour market. An extreme example was the former wife of a titled land owner currently working as a domestic cleaner, but we found former secretaries employed in schools as kitchen staff or cleaners, who had found that they were unable to manage to learn the skills required as the result of technological advances in office work.

This analysis of female employment after divorce is supported both by the study by Martin (1984) referred to above and a research report for the University of Warwick Institute for Employment Research by Elias and Main.[6] Both show that women's work patterns are determined overwhelmingly by two variables: their own age and the age of their children. A divorced woman seeking re-employment after many years of child caregiving is in no different position, vis- -vis the labour market, than a married woman. However, as the latter report in particular illustrates, women returning to the labour market experience 'skill-downgrading' to the extent that one in five who were working part time in low or unskilled personal-service occupations had previously enjoyed a more highly-skilled full-time job ten years earlier. If this woman is divorced and has not reconstituted with another wage earner, her economic position will be very much worse than a married woman returning to work, as she has only her own earnings to support her. This evidence also undermines the policy concerns of many recent reforms of the maintenance obligation. These were expressly seen as being a response to an imagined excessive reliance of women in the long term, on maintenance payments. Legislation has therefore sought to introduce incentives for these women to acquire self-sufficiency.[7] The reality seems to be that this is precisely what they do seek to acquire. But the dice are loaded. The present goal of self-sufficiency is as futile as the now abandoned objective of keeping a divorced family at its previous standard of living.

(b) The extent and impact of maintenance payments

We now turn to consider the relationship between the woman's own earning capacity and that of her husband, represented in the form of maintenance payments. It is here where one of the starkest contrasts between the childless divorces and the other categories becomes apparent. In the childless cases, we found only five (11 per cent) in which a court order had been made for continuing support after divorce, and only one (2 per cent) where there was a voluntary arrangement for this. By contrast, continuing support orders had been made in ninety-seven (55 per cent) and voluntary arrangements in a further twenty-eight (10 per cent) of the divorces involving independent children. Only one of our long-term mothers whose children had become independent by the time of separation had an order made in her favour, but this lapsed after a year and no attempt had been made to enforce it, as the husband had retired. Even more strikingly, if we look at the position at the time of interview, in *none* of the childless cases did we find income transfer taking place at that time. Three of the orders had never been kept and one had expired. In the children divorces, on the other hand, income transfers were still taking place in 36 per cent of the cases. In many, of course, the children had grown up by the time of the interview, so if we narrow this group down and look only at those cases where a dependent child was still living with the mother at time of interview, and she had not remarried or begun cohabiting with another man, if we include mortgage payments, we find that income transfers were being made in 68 per cent of these cases.

Once again, the long-term mothers are in an intermediate position. Of the eleven who had no children under sixteen, no money was changing hands at the time of interview save in one case of a disabled woman. Four orders had been made for children, two of which had never been paid; the other two had expired when the children reached eighteen. Of the eleven who had children over sixteen but also a child between twelve and sixteen, five were receiving regular maintenance, in three cases for the children only. It seems clear that, as the children reached majority, income transfers were stopping, leaving the former caregivers to fall back on their own resources, or those of the state. Only two of the eleven with adult children were just above the poverty line (140 per cent of supplementary benefit entitlement), and none approached average income. All the others were below the poverty line. All were in employment, except two (one disabled and one retired).

The incidence of income transfer after divorce was not merely a function of the length of the marriage. It is true that the childless divorces tended to end shorter marriages. Sixty-eight per cent of them had lasted under five years, compared to 32 per cent of the marriages which had produced children. But the few occasions where support was ordered or agreed between the childless bore no relation to the length of the marriage. In the nineteen cases where no arrangements were made for transfer of income to the caregiving parents of children or children under eighteen at divorce, the reasons appeared to be related to ability to pay, rather than to family circumstances. Ten of the nineteen men were not earning, two had left the country, two wives claimed to earn more than their ex-husbands, one case was not yet settled, and four were unclear.

Other research has confirmed the contrast between childless and children divorces in this respect. In Scotland, Doig (1982)[8] reported that *claims* for periodical allowance were made in only 18 per cent of cases where there were no children (defined as children present under sixteen), and stated that in 46 per cent of cases involving claims for periodical allowance, the judge awarded nothing. On the other hand, claims for periodical allowance were made in 42 per cent of children cases, and more significantly, claims for aliment (child support) were made in 65 per cent of them. Awards were made in 95 per cent of the aliment claims. Gibson's survey of divorce decrees granted in England and Wales in 1971 showed that less than 18 per cent of childless wives had a maintenance order at the time of divorce, whereas a maintenance order of some kind existed in 72 per cent of cases where the wives had dependent children at the time of the divorce.[9]

Nor can the absence of provision for continuing support in the childless cases be accounted for by the making, in those cases, of provision in alternative forms, such as settlement of the home or other assets. We have already described the position regarding the home and our evidence on that, and on other matters concerning asset distribution, does not indicate the use of any such devices. Our findings concerning the use of legal services confirm this sharp contrast between childless and children divorces. Sixty-one per cent of the former respondents had consulted a lawyer, compared to 87 per cent of those with children. Almost all the women with children had done this. The childless seldom received legal aid (only 9 per cent) whereas 63 per cent of those with children did do so. The consequence, however, was that 70 per cent of the latter escaped meeting charges personally, the costs falling substantially on the legal aid fund. A very small number (4 per cent) had to meet very heavy legal bills. However, usually the amount was less than £200. The conclusion we can draw is of the relative simplicity of childless divorces. The parties rarely concern themselves with complexities involving continuing support or accommodation. The only significant transaction will be the sale of the house or the purchase by the husband of the joint legal interest of the other. In only 6 per cent of cases was a solicitor consulted about other assets.

The most significant set of circumstances in which maintenance payments may have an impact on family income is therefore where the mother is caring for dependent children. Some form of maintenance on their account was, as we have seen, paid in two-thirds (68 per cent) of these cases in our sample. Hitherto, the significance of maintenance payments has been assessed on the basis of the amounts ordered to be paid and the degree of compliance with such orders. The Finer Committee in particular were very unimpressed with the sums ordered by magistrates, pointing out that they were much lower than the recipients' supplementary benefit entitlement and that the higher they were the quicker they fell into arrears.[10] Doig[11] found evidence that child support orders in Scotland were 'likely' to be paid in one-quarter of cases, but observed that there was no indication one way or the other for nearly half of the orders. It does appear, however, looking at our data based on the reports of those entitled to payment, that the degree to which some resources move across families is not inconsiderable.

The amounts which are so transferred are, of course, another matter. They are often very small: half (n = 14) below £10 per week, a quarter (n = 7) between £10 and £20, and only a quarter (n = 8) above £20. But in over half the cases these payments had been received for over five years (15 per cent for over ten, and 42 per cent for six to ten years), thus adding up, over time, to considerable sums. Indeed, these amounts can represent a significant part of the receiving household's income, as Table 6.1 shows. For one in five of the single mothers with respect to whom maintenance was paid, the payments represented less than one-tenth of their income, but for half of them they constituted between one-tenth and one-third of their income and for one-quarter, more than one-third. For seven per cent, maintenance made up more than half their household income. But this represents only two of all the forty-seven lone mothers with children in our sample (4.2 per cent), corresponding closely with the rough national estimates that maintenance forms the major source of income for only six per cent of single parent families.[12]

However, a very important qualification must be made to the picture

Table 6.1. *Maintenance payments as a percentage of caregiver's household income*

Percentage of household income	One-parent families (n = 30)		Reconstituted families (n = 30)	
	No.	%	No.	%
Up to 5 6–10	4	20	10	63
	2		9	
11–20	9	50	6	24
21–30	6		1	
31–50	5	24	1	10
Over 50	2		2	
Not known	2	6	1	3

thus represented. For, while our information indicated that these were the amounts which were actually paid, in seventeen (57 per cent) of these instances the maintenance paid did not affect the caregiver's household income at all. This was because she was in receipt of supplementary benefit, so the payment went either directly to the state or reduced the amount of benefit to which she was entitled.

It is here that we see a different kind of poverty trap. Twelve of the seventeen cases mentioned above were women who were not employed. Although they attracted maintenance payments, this was of no direct benefit to them. The residual resource of their former spouse's earning capacity, to the extent that it was available to them at all, was directed at replenishing the state, not improving their own or their children's position. Five of these seventeen women were in part-time work, using their earnings to supplement their social security entitlements. Single parents on supplementary benefit who work part time are permitted to keep up to £12 per week of their earnings (the Tapered Earnings Disregard) without deduction of benefit.[13] But the disregard does not extend to maintenance, which in the case of these five women, was of benefit only to the state. In some cases the women were attempting to live on their own resources without recourse to the state. Two of the total of twenty who were not employed lived on maintenance and child benefit, both of them below our estimate of their supplementary benefit entitlement. This was true also for the three part-time workers who received maintenance rather than supplementary benefit. There is clearly no incentive to forgo basic social security entitlements in favour of maintenance. Indeed, the availability of maintenance might be seen to have been disadvantageous to these individuals.

Table 6.2 shows the position of the women who combined full-time earnings with maintenance payments. The small numbers involved should be noted. Two of the nine were considerably (between 45.7 and at least 84.5 per cent) better off than they would have been had they relied on supplementary benefit augmented by part-time earnings, (assuming they would achieve the maximum £12 benefit of the disregard), one-third were hardly better off at all, and the rest had improved on that notional position by between 15.8 and 20.3 per cent. In addition, account should be taken of the costs of full time employment (such as eating out, travel and child-minding expenses). However, it appears that the receipt of maintenance payments may have a directly beneficial impact in some of these cases. Because the recipient is in full-time work, and accordingly not in receipt of supplementary benefit, the maintenance payment actually enhances her income, in some cases raising it above (although

Table 6.2. *Actual income of single mothers working full time (n = 9, omitting woman receiving study grant), compared to their supplementary benefit entitlement and notional income if working part time, showing the significance of maintenance*

Case	(a) Supplementary-benefit entitlement	(b) Notional maximum income from part-time earnings and supp. ben.	(c) Income without maintenance	(d) Maintenance received	(e) Amount by which total income exceeds (b)
	£	£	£	£	%
1	47	59	66	5	20.3
2	50	62	64	8	16.1
3	63	75	67	10	2.6
4	63	75	80	0	6.6
5	68	80	47	35	2.5
6	47	59	86	0	45.7
7	63	75	88	0	17.3
8	70	82	89	6	15.8
9	60	72	unknown	133	above 84.5

not usually a great deal above) the amount she would have earned had she relied on supplementary benefit and part-time earnings. In sum, maintenance payments are usually only of direct benefit to the payer's children if the caregiver is in full-time employment. Whether such a solution is in the ultimate interests of the children is doubtful. The advantages of increased income may be purchased at the expense of their mother's care (and possibly health) and in any case dissipated in increased child care expenses. The poorer the mother is, especially if she is unemployed or only partially employed, the less likely it is that she will get any benefit from the maintenance payment, although the proportion of her actual income which that payment represents is higher than it would be if her own income was greater. (See Table 6.3.) These are issues of supreme importance, which we shall address in detail in our ultimate proposals for reconsideration of the role of maintenance and state provision.

Before leaving the position of women with dependent children, we should consider the role which maintenance payments play once the woman reconstitutes a two-adult family with another partner. This event seems to constitute a significant occasion for the termination of maintenance payments. The proportion of mothers in this position reporting

Table 6.3. *Maintenance as percentage of household income for all women with children receiving maintenance, by level of household income*

Maintenance as % of household income	Household income up to 100% supplementary benefit	Household income of 100–200% supplementary benefit (no cases had incomes over 200%)
up to 5	6	9
6–10	5	6
11–20	6	7
Over 20	11	6
Not known	2	2
Total	30	30

payments was 47 per cent, compared to 68 per cent of those who had not reconstituted. The percentage is still reasonably high, but the difference from the single parent families is important in view of the fact that the legal obligation upon the absent parent to support his *children* (apart from his former spouse) does not lapse on her remarriage. The reduction may therefore reflect a recognition among families that the *de facto* obligation transfers to the new breadwinner and day-to-day parent, especially in the case of younger children. The amounts that were paid to reconstituted families were also lower than those paid to single mothers (70 per cent were under £10 and only 13 per cent over £20); but, with characteristic irony, since these families were not on supplementary benefit, the payments were more likely in their case to have an actual impact on their household income.

(c) Current resources of the absent parent

Twenty-nine men in our sample had children of their first marriage living in another household, of whom twelve currently had other children in their present household and seventeen had not. Of these twenty-nine, nine men were not paying maintenance regularly. Five of these men were unemployed at the time of interview, and one also said that access was in dispute. Two had stopped paying maintenance when their former wife had remarried and in one case maintenance was not paid because custody of the child was shared. It seems clear that unemployment was a major cause of inability to pay maintenance. Furthermore, one in four (twelve out of forty-seven) of the husbands of our single mothers were unemployed at the time of the divorce. It has been suggested that this kind of unemployment may have been sought by the men to avoid their maintenance obligations. But it is at least as likely that marital problems and employment problems develop side by side. This association between marital breakdown and disruption of work performance has been recorded by the General Household Survey for some years,[14] and is discussed by Daniel (1981) in the context of entry into unemployment.[15]

Twenty fathers of children under sixteen were paying maintenance (nine of the twelve with other children in the household, and eleven of the seventeen without). The payments made are described as a percentage of household income for men with and without children in the present household, and are shown in Table 6.4.

Table 6.4. *Fathers paying maintenance (n = 20)*

Maintenance as % of household income	With children in household	Without children in household	All payers
Up to 5	4	2	6
6–10	2	4	6
Over 10	2	5	7
Not known	1	0	1
Total	9	11	20

The men without children in their present household were more likely to pay over 10 per cent of their household income to their absent children, than the men with a second family. The part such payments play in the household economy of the maintenance payer appears far less significant than in the receiver's household economy. For only just over one-third of the men (35 per cent) did the transfer represent more than 10 per cent of their household income, whereas Table 6.1 showed that maintenance constituted over 10 per cent of the income of over half of all the women, and indeed did so for 74 per cent of the women living alone with their children (though not always directly affecting their ultimate income).

Looking more closely at the financial circumstances of the men who paid maintenance, Table 6.5 shows the distribution of the proportion of maintenance paid, related to the payer's household income between payers' households of different income levels, of all men who had at least one child (whether their own or step) under sixteen in their current household (caregiving men). This enables us to see whether men who were being called upon to support their absent children had a different financial profile from all divorced men currently supporting children in their household.

Table 6.5. *Maintenance paid as a percentage of household income, by income as a percentage of supplementary benefit entitlement*

Maintenance as % of house- hold income	Up to 100	100–200	201–300	Over 300	Not known	Total No.	%
Up to 5	0	3	2	1	0	6	30
6–10	0	4	0	2	0	6	30
Over 10	1	3	2	1	0	7	35
Not known	0	0	0	0	1	1	5
All men paying maintenance (n = 20)	1 (5%)	10 (50%)	4 (20%)	4 (20%)	1 (5%)	20	100
All custodial men (n = 45)	10 (22%)	22 (49%)	6 (14%)	6 (14%)	1 (2%)	45	100

It can be seen that, while 55 per cent of the payers had below average incomes (i.e. under 200 per cent supplementary benefit entitlement), 71 per cent of all caregiving men were in that position. But this was almost entirely due to the fact that men under supplementary benefit level do not pay maintenance. Nevertheless, 40 per cent of payers had above average incomes compared to 28 per cent of the others. The men who pay are slightly better off as a group than all the caregiving men. But, as Table 6.5 also shows, the proportion of income handed over varied very little with income. This raises the question whether the fathers with above-average incomes (both those now paying maintenance and those not) had resources which might more readily be transferred to their absent children? We could calculate how much in excess of average income (i.e. 200 per cent supplementary benefit entitlement) were the ten fathers with above average incomes who had children under sixteen living in another household after they had paid their maintenance. Two of these men also had children in their present household. After paying their current maintenance, one had £2 surplus and the other £7. But of the eight with no children in their present household, all but two had over £10 surplus, sometimes considerably more, after paying existing maintenance (Table 6.6). These figures represent their income only at one point in time, and these men's incomes may vary over time. But it seems possible that for many men who do not have children in their present household, increased maintenance could be paid without depressing the payers below an average standard of living. We do not know the standard of living of the children outside the household of these particular men, but, if it were below the average standard, the discrepancy between them is hard to justify.

Table 6.6. *Income of caregiving fathers without children in present household, in excess of 200 per cent supplementary benefit level, after payment at maintenance for absent children*

		Maintenance paid £	Surplus to 200% supplementary benefit £
Remarried men	1	5	8
	2	0	73
	3	14	29
	4	0	13
Men alone	1	0	36
	2	10	42
	3	6	36
	4	4	8

III. Resources of Reconstituted Families

Reconstitution, while not a necessary event after breakdown of the original family, usually brings with it significant economic benefits to a parent who was formerly living alone with the children. This much is clear from the data we have reviewed in this and the previous chapter. But we must also ask another question about reconstitution. What implications does it have on the resources of the maintenance payer? We are not at this point confronting the normative problem as to how far the economic benefits which a new partner brings should enure to the advantage of the maintenance payer's former family. We are simply concerned with the factual question of trying to assess the resources of those families and the impact which maintenance payments have on them.

A partial view of the picture which our data revealed was indicated in the preceding section. We saw (Table 6.6.) that, after their maintenance had been paid, most men *who had not reformed a family containing children* were left with a household income appreciably in excess of the average, *whether they had remarried or not*. Indeed, there was no difference in the degree of this surplus between the remarried and the non-remarried men. The implication is clearly that the fact of reconstitution (for example, by remarriage) makes less impact on their standard of living than does the introduction of children. However, this evidence refers only to the men who were paying maintenance who, as Table 6.5 indicated, tend to be better off in any case. We need to look at the reconstituted families and to compare their economic profile both with single-parent households and households in the general population. Table 6.7 shows that the reconstituted households are considerably better off than the single parent households, but somewhat worse off than the average household. Why were the reconstituted households living at a lower standard than the average? It does not appear to be due to a drain on resources due to maintenance payments. We therefore divided the reconstituted families into those above (n = 63) and those below (n = 29) our poverty line of 140 per cent of supplementary-benefit level. Table 6.8 suggests the reasons why the poorer group were in that position. The number of unemployed men among them was three times the then national rate and there was a lower proportion of women working and producing a second income. These families were also a little more likely than the better off group to contain three or more children.

Table 6.7. *Present situation of single and reconstituted families with the available indications for the general population*

	Head of household in full-time employment %	Housing status owner-occupiers %	Percentage with household income above 140% supplementary-benefit entitlement %
Single parents	23	29	20
Reconstituted parents	83	53	63
Households in the general population	88*	55	71†

* *Social Trends* (HMSO, 1982) pp. 72, 151, referring to 1980 data † Layard (1978), *Royal Commission on the Distribution of Income and Wealth*, Background Paper No. 6 (London, HMSO)

Table 6.8. *Possible factors contributing to income levels of reconstituted families*

	Below 140% supplementary-benefit (n = 29)	At or above 140% supplementary-benefit entitlement (n = 63)
Percentage of women working	28	46
Percentage of men not working	40	6
Percentage with three or more children	31	21
Percentage paying or receiving maintenance	38	33

Conclusions

We set out below in summary form the principal findings described in this and the previous chapter.

(a)   Childless divorces are significantly different from divorces where dependent children are present in the following respects.

(i) Court orders for continuing maintenance were made in only 10 per cent of childless divorces compared to 55 per cent of children divorces.

(ii) In none of the childless cases was income transfer still taking place at the time of interview, compared to 36 per cent of all the children cases and two-thirds of those where the mother was still looking after dependent children by herself.

(iii) Childless couples occupying public sector housing usually left the home on divorce whereas the home continued to be occupied by one of the parties to a children divorce; while owner-occupied homes were equally likely to be sold in the case of childless and children divorces. If the house was not sold, the husband usually remained in it if the divorce was childless, whereas the wife stayed in half the cases where there were children. If the wife was joined by a new partner, she would move to accommodation provided by him.

(iv) Sixty-one per cent of the childless cases saw a lawyer, compared to 87 per cent of those with children. Only nine per cent of the childless received legal aid, compared to 63 per cent of those with children.

(v) The household net disposable income of men and women

divorcees of childless marriages was, at interview, comparable to that of the population as a whole; the equivalent incomes of divorcees of 'children' divorces, whether or not they had remarried, was well below that.

(*b*)   The household net disposable income of a divorced parent living alone with dependent children was considerably lower than that of the parent without children in the household; the income of families 'reconstituted' by remarriage or cohabitation fell somewhere between the two. This finding is echoed by our data on the long-term effects on educational attainment of the children of divorcing parents, where remarriage mitigated but did not remove the effect of marital breakdown.

(*c*)   Where maintenance was paid to a female single parent family it rarely had any impact on the total household income of that family unless the woman was working full time, when it may have helped to bring the income above the level it would be if she worked part time and received supplementary benefit; the gains were unevenly spread, but generally small.

(*d*)   The amounts of maintenance transferred were very low, but nevertheless could form a significant percentage of the recipient family's income. In half of cases it was between 11 and 30 per cent and in one-quarter it was over 30 per cent. But many families did not receive any of this potential benefit because payment went to the state to offset supplementary benefit.

(*e*)   Maintenance paid by fathers formed a much lower percentage of their own household income. It exceeded 10 per cent for only one-third of the payers. But for men who had reformed families with children, these payments could not have been substantially increased without reducing their standard of living below that of the average family. However, where dependent children had not been introduced into the man's new family (or he lived alone) their standard of living remained relatively well above the average, despite the effects of making maintenance payments.

(*f*)   As lone caregiving mothers grew older, and the children gradually became independent, child support payments dwindled, then ceased. During this period the mothers increasingly attempted to return to employment, or more extensive employment. But their earning capacity had been devastatingly impaired by the interruption in their employment pattern.

Notes

1. J. E. Todd and L. M. Jones (1972), *Matrimonial Property* (London, HMSO); A. J. Manners and I. Rauta (1981), *Family Property in Scotland* (London, HMSO).
2. See *United Kingdom in Figures* (1981) (Government Statistical Service, HMSO).
3. Jennie Popay, Leslie Rimmer and Chris Rossiter (1983), *One Parent Families* (Study Commission on the Family), p. 49. G. Davis, A. MacLeod and Mervyn Murch (1983), 'Divorce: Who Supports the Family?' 13 *Family Law*, 217–24 found an almost identical pattern to ours in their differently collected sample.
4. Jean Martin (1984), *Women and Employment* (Office of Population, Censuses and Surveys, London, HMSO), pp. 13, 15; Popay *et al.* (1983), p. 49.
5. See note 3.
6. Peter Elias and Brian Main, *Women's Working Lives: Evidence from the National Training Survey* (University of Warwick Institute for Employment Research, no date).
7. Above, pp. 49–51.
8. B. Doig (1982), *The Nature and Scale of Aliment and Financial Provision on Divorce in Scotland* (Edinburgh, Central Research Unit, Scottish Office).
9. Personal communication.
10. *Report of the Committee on One-Parent Families* (Finer Report) (1974) Cmnd. 5629, vol. 1, paras, 101–4.
11. Doig (1982), p. 28.
12. Popay *et al.* (1983), p. 47.
13. Albert Weale, Jonathan Bradshaw, Alan Maynard and David Piachaud (1984), *Lone Mothers, Paid Work and Social Security* (Occasional Paper in Social Administration 77, Bedford Square Press), examining the operation of the disregard, shows that the mean net gain achieved by women through the disregard is £3.29 a week.
14. See *General Household Survey 1982* (London, HMSO).
15. W. Daniel (1981), *The Unemployed Flow* (London, Policy Studies Institute).

7. The Principles of Child Support

In this chapter and the next we attempt an evaluation of the principles which should govern post-divorce maintenance. These are not merely technical matters. At every turn we confront fundamental questions concerning the ideology of family responsibility, the relationship between the individual and the state, and the demarcation between the roles of the legislature and the judiciary. We cannot pretend to be neutral on such issues and we will deploy various normative arguments. But we will also try to elucidate what the central issues are which must be confronted, and resolved, if a coherent policy is to be achieved. Our conclusions will seek to achieve a balance between competing interests and values as assessed in the light of our research findings.

I. Relationship Between Child Support and Maintenance of Former Spouse

We start with the question of child support. The data which we have reviewed in the preceding chapters establish that, after divorce, serious problems of continuing support arise mainly when one or both of the adults continues to have the care of a child who has not become economically independent of the household. This alone justifies a separate examination of this area. But we believe there are further, analytic, reasons for doing this.

How far a former spouse should owe a continuing obligation to support the other is a matter which has generated considerable controversy in recent years and, as was shown in Chapter 3, has been subject to extensive legislative and judicial attention. We will consider some of these problems later. At present we wish to argue that where a former spouse is caring for a child, those issues become, or should become, superseded by the application of principles properly applicable to child support. Suppose, for example, it is held that in principle there should be no continuing obligation towards a spouse, or that, in a particular case, such obligation was rebutted by the 'misconduct' of the spouse. It will not follow that there should be no obligation towards a child for whom the spouse is caring, although we may observe, in passing, that when courts have discounted for 'misconduct' they have paid scant attention to the impact of the reduction on the living standards of the children involved.[1] If the caregiving spouse has no income (ignoring for the moment state provision) the extent to which the child is provided for will depend on the degree to which the obligation (if any) of the other spouse towards him is carried out. Such provision might be confined to the costs of the necessaries of bare sustenance of the child, but this will seldom be realistic because the child will require to be housed, warmed, and attended. In so far as provision is made for these things, they must entail provision for the caregiver. If they are things which should, in principle, be supplied to the child by the parent, they must override the injunction against providing for the caregiving spouse. Similarly, it may be held that a former spouse need support the other only if that other cannot acquire income from employment. But if the other has the care of a child, the application of the rule has obvious implications for the type, and possibly the quality, of care which the child is likely to receive. Looked at from the point of view of the support and care the child is entitled to receive, the obligation on the caregiver to seek employment must be subsidiary to the child's entitlement.

There are many ways in which English post-divorce maintenance law recognizes the subsidiarity of an adult's entitlement to that of the children. The clearest instances have arisen in relation to the arrangements made regarding the matrimonial home. There was a time when the law gave untrammelled effect to the property rights of a divorced husband, permitting him to turn his wife out of the home, even if that meant turning out his children as well. Indeed, this process was seen as 'inevitable'.[2] After the introduction of the reformed divorce law in 1971, which brought with it extensive new powers for the courts to rearrange the property of the adult parties, it emerged that the dominant concern of the courts was to secure a home for the children, which of course effectively also provided housing for whichever adult was caring for them.[3] Although the property transfer would be made in favour of the adult and not the children, it is clear that the adult received the benefit in the capacity of child caregiver, not as a former spouse. What should be done with the house when the children became independent, raised a separate set of problems, which will be considered in the next chapter.

As far as income support is concerned, traditional maintenance law has sought to deal separately with the claims of the former spouse and the children. In Chapter 2 we argued that the current basis for distinguishing between the two elements in the award reflects extrinsic considerations (such as fiscal advantages) which have no rational connection with the formal attribution of the elements of the award to the adult and to the children. At this point we would assert a stronger claim. We would argue that there can be no rational basis for distinguishing the two elements.

It might be objected that a distinction can be drawn between the costs of maintaining a child (food, clothing, education, sundries) and provision for the child's care-giver. Household income might indeed be broken down in this fashion. However, it would be irrational to distinguish the *reason* for supporting the care-giver from the *reason* for meeting the expenses of the child. For if there is an obligation (on some third party) to meet the latter, this must include a duty to maintain the means by which they are administered. The obligation to provide one cannot rest on principles different from those requiring support for the other. It would be irrational to maintain that a parent has an obligation to ensure that his child is provided with the necessaries of life while denying, for example on the ground of misconduct, any obligation to provide for the sustenance of the care-giver. It follows from this that the elements constituting the child's economic well-being are indivisible. Food, housing, physical protection, care and attention, among other things, all combine to determine the standard at which the child benefits from available resources. In short, all these factors constitute the child's standard of living.[4]

The identification of the child's standard of living with that of the caregiving parent was implicitly recognized by the Law Commission in 1969 when it proposed that, after divorce, a former spouse should be under a prima facie obligation to maintain the other at the same level he or she would have enjoyed had the marriage not broken down.[5] For the Commission also proposed that the maintenance obligation towards a child should be set so as to place him 'in the financial position in which the child would have been if the marriage had not broken down and each of those parties[6] had properly discharged his or her financial obligations and responsibilities towards him'.[7] While the Commission supported the adoption of this principle in relation to the adult parties by reference to existing case law, no such justification existed in its application to children. Indeed, the incoherence of existing practice in relation to child support would have precluded attempts to justify it on the basis of current authority.[8] The Commission merely stated, having set out the principle in relation to the adults, that 'similarly' such a principle should apply to children.[9] Equally, when, in 1984, the principle was repealed with regard to the adults, it was also removed with respect to children.[10] It clearly would have been untenable to have done otherwise. Yet the major argument for removing the principle in relation to adults, namely, that it embodied a theory of a continuing obligation to support a former spouse after divorce which was inconsistent with modern divorce law,[11] cannot apply to the child support obligation. Nevertheless, it was primarily this argument which precipitated the demise of the principle as regards adults[12] and with it, without further comment, its application to children.

If we cannot separate the principles on which maintenance for a child and its caregiver should be based, we need to decide in such cases whether the obligation is to be determined by principles relevant to the adult parties or principles relevant to the child's entitlement towards adults. We have already discussed the uncertainties surrounding modern developments relating to the post-divorce obligations between the adults. We will return to them later. If a clearer set of principles can be developed regarding the child support obligation, it may be that, in cases where the adult claimant is caring for children, the principles of child support will be sufficient to conclude the matter. If any such principles point to a higher support obligation than could be based on the adult's claim alone, then the latter's claim becomes irrelevant. That claim would be relevant only if, the claim by the children being exhausted, additional grounds could still be found for a claim by the other adult. Whether such grounds can reasonably arise is a matter for Chapter 8. We need first to examine the nature and extent of the child's claim.

II. The state obligation

The following discussion is premissed on the assumption that, in principle, each of a child's natural parents is under an obligation to support the child. Even if this is accepted as a workable hypothesis, attempts might be made to limit its application by reference to factors such as the extent to which the parents assumed the obligation or even their reliance on the actions of others (whether the other parent or third parties), to ensure that conception did not take place.[13] We regard these issues as peripheral to our task. It is essential, when confronting the highly complex issues of child support, to address the 'central' case, for unless an acceptable approach to this can be found, arguments about exceptional situations will lack a firm point of reference.

Radical social theory might seek to displace the parental obligation entirely, substituting an obligation on the community at large. The justification for such a move would be simple. Children, it would be claimed, form the human investment of any community. The community as a whole, therefore, owes to all its children an obligation of support.[14] It is clear that, to a large extent, such arguments have been accepted at a political level. The availability of supplementary benefit payments for persons without adequate means of support, into which additions are built for the benefit of children, is partly a realization of this claim. Additional state provision for children, whether by way of cash, as in child benefit,[15] or in kind, as provided in health and educational services, or in housing policy, supplements this principle. However, it is clear that in most Western societies state provision, except as an instrument of last resort in cases of severe deprivation, covers only selective (though often important) areas of a child's life. It remains true, with the intact family as much as for the separated family, that the child takes his standard of living primarily from that of his parents. To the extent, of course, that the community may fail to provide basic services for children, the more vital become the family's resources to ensuring their well-being.

This follows inexorably from the organizational basis of child-rearing in Western societies. Typically, children are raised in families. The family is the agency through which the community's children receive their primary economic support. If the state were to assume responsibility for the standard of living of all children, it would thereby be committed to doing the same for their families. This would mean a commitment to uphold a standard of living for *all* families at a reasonably high level and a reduction of the economic 'space' in which the standard of living of the children would be subject to variation according to individual family incomes and resources. The economic implications of such a course could, of course, be avoided by abolishing family-based child rearing and bringing up all children in state-financed settings, leaving adults to achieve their own standard of living according to the current economic conditions. It is not our purpose to pronounce on the merits of such solutions. We point to them only to bring out the constraints within which child support law operates. For the purposes of the study, we will assume that neither of these options is a practicable alternative. We need to assume a system of economic and social organization within which a substantial factor in determining a child's standard of living is to be found in the resources generated in his immediate family.

It is, of course, a consequence of this fact that, as the data we have reviewed earlier demonstrated, children suffer economic deprivation when their parents separate. If that happens, the assumption which we can usually make while the family remains a geographic unit, that a child will share in the resources and living standards of both his parents, can no longer be made, especially if the more economically powerful family member removes himself from the group. Economic resources must be visibly transferred from that individual to the unit containing the child if the child is to participate in them to any degree. The context is therefore appropriate for the interposition of agreements or orders to determine the extent of these transfers.

It may be argued that it is inappropriate to attempt to maintain a child's standard of living in this way. A child living apart from a parent cannot share the benefits of basic living costs, such as housing. His costs are no longer marginal to that parent. And the evidence shows this to be true. One major income earner is seldom able to support two establishments at a reasonable standard. It is therefore difficult to resist the conclusion that the child whose family is broken should have prima facie recourse against the community to supply the standard of living which that community owes to its children. Yet Western countries have been tenacious in retaining the ideology that a child should look first to its parents for the retention of its living standards, even after the collapse of the family unit. The state, it is true, has been ready to move in as an ultimate guarantor against an unacceptable level of poverty, but even in this situation assistance has frequently been conditional on the instigation of legal machinery by the child's caregiver to extract support from the other parent.[16] With the acceleration of divorce in the mid-twentieth century, and the consequential growth in reconstituted families, Western legal systems began to attenuate the extent of the obligation of a former main breadwinner towards the family from which he was separated, out of concern for the interests of his later-acquired dependants.[17] Such developments heightened the significance of state support for the first family. Yet it often remains that the state is seen as a reserve resource, acting only if recourse against the absent parent fails. This is so even in Sweden, where the state will pay a maintenance advance for each child of a single parent family only if the liable parent has not complied with a judgment or agreement.[18]

In 1974 the Finer Committee made a recommendation which, had it been accepted, would have produced a significant shift in the social perception of the community's obligation towards its children. It proposed that a guaranteed maintenance allowance should be payable to all one-parent families, irrespective of how the loss of the parent occurred. The state would have the right to reclaim contributions from the liable relative, but the primary recourse of the child and his caregiver for support would be against the state. Although this proposal was rejected by the government on financial grounds,[19] the Committee's observations led to a change in the practice whereby the supplementary benefit authorities either 'encouraged' or 'required' single parent claimants to take maintenance proceedings against their separated partner, before paying them supplementary benefit.[20] This, however, only goes part of the way towards the re-orientation of the child support obligation which the full implementation of the Committee's proposals would have brought about. Supplementary benefit is essentially a basic subsistence allowance, representing the official calculation of the ultimate poverty level below which it is deemed no citizen (or family) should fall. Where a family is in danger of sinking thus far, first recourse may now be had to the state, whether the family is broken by separation (or any other cause) or not. Supplementary benefit payments, even if boosted by child benefit and other social welfare provision, cannot be considered as a substitute for family support as a general means for the provision of an adequate standard of living for the community's children. The Finer Committee's guaranteed maintenance allowance came closer to fulfilling that function. The level of the allowance was not to be equivalent to any other social security benefit, but was to 'make most one-parent families rather better off than they would be on supplementary benefit'. It would 'in the normal way give a clear advantage over supplementary benefit for one-parent families with no other income'.[21]

On what principle did the Committee rest its decision as to the level of the proposed benefit? The Committee appealed to the principle that the benefit should give a lone parent 'a real choice between working and staying at home to look after the children'.[22] In a era of unemployment one might add the consideration that the parent who stays home perforce should not be significantly prejudiced thereby. But a parent who obtained employment would remain entitled to the benefit, on a diminishing scale, until the earnings reached the level of average full-time male earnings.[23] The proposal effectively created a new living standard, somewhat above the official 'poverty' level but below the 'average' family wage, to which all the community's children would be entitled if the family support system failed in their case. There might, on this scheme, still remain some children worse off than these, whose intact families were not generating an equivalent standard of living. Such compromises are inherent in a social system which distributes economic responsibility for supporting children between families and the community. The bases upon which they are struck require careful consideration, and we will return to the issue later.[24]

Although the United Kingdom has refused up to now to take the step indicated by the Finer Committee, New Zealand has done so. In 1973 that country introduced Domestic Purposes Benefits payable to all 'solo' parents with the care of one or more children. The level of the benefit is equivalent to that payable to widows. In this way, the children of families broken by death are treated in the same way as those of families broken by separation.[25] The recipient need show no inability to work, so could choose full-time child care rather than employment. However, after a disregard, earnings are taken into account, as are any maintenance payments. In 1981, the relationship between payment of the benefit and collection of maintenance from the absent parents, was restructured. No longer was recourse against that parent to be a precondition to the payment. All that is now necessary is that the 'liable relative' should be 'identified in law'. The payments may then be made, leaving the social security authorities to pursue the liable relative for a contribution calculated according to a series of statutory formulae.[26] While payments are made, any liability under a maintenance order is suspended. It is, however, open to a claimant to seek an order against the liable relative, and this may be useful if (she) is contemplating employment, with the consequence of coming off the state benefit. As we have observed in relation to our data, maintenance payments can be of real benefit to recipient households if added to the earnings of the lone parent. However, a New Zealand commentator has observed that 'for most beneficiaries there will be little point in suing for maintenance', and added that one can now 'surmise with greater confidence the end of spousal maintenance'.[27]

While such a prediction may be premature (at least as regards child support), the New Zealand system marks a decisive break with traditional thinking about child support. No longer is it assumed that the child should look primarily to the resources of an absent parent as a determinant of its living standards. The state has settled what these should be, and provides a uniform criterion for all children of broken families. Recourse may be had against the resources of the absent parent, but this is not done in order to support the child. The main reason is to raise revenue for the state.[28] The motives for exacting this revenue from the 'liable relative' are complex. They are certainly related to the ethos that parents, and sometimes other family members, owe a moral obligation to support the family's children where they can.[29] To this can be added fears that 'irresponsible' social behaviour would be encouraged if the implications of the procreative aspects of sexual activity could be avoided.[30] The right of recourse by the state, therefore, is not performed in order to provide support for the child from the resources of the absent parent, but as an exercise in raising revenue and attempting behaviour control, akin to penal law. It follows that, where the only beneficiary of a maintenance payment is the state, the state should not enforce it as if it were simply a private obligation, as happens under present practice where enforcement proceedings need to be authorized by the nominal payee (the former wife) effectively acting as proxy for the state.[31]

We have already stated that it seems to us inescapable that the community should assume the primary responsibility for making provision for the upbringing of a child at a reasonable standard where the child's family has collapsed. How that standard is to be set is a matter of some complexity. It might be argued, in theory, that the level should be that which the child would have enjoyed had the family remained unbroken. The difficulties of achieving this in practice rule it out as a solution, however theoretically attractive it may seem. A strong argument can be made that, if a uniform level is to be applied to all broken families, the standard should be that of the average, two-parent family. In this way policy would assure, as far as it could, that the economic consequences of the breakdown would not operate so as to disadvantage the child against other children in the community. Apart from the costs of such a solution, objection is likely to be found in the fact that it would leave many children of broken families better off than children of intact families, perhaps even raising them to a standard higher than they would have enjoyed if the family had continued. This could be seen as both an incentive to family breakdown and a disincentive to family reconstitution. We must not be taken to be convinced by such objections. Family breakdown visits many other hardships on the parents other than purely economic ones and we should not too easily assume that parents will be induced to separate by modest economic attractions.[32] But the political restraints against such a solution are in any event likely to be too great to permit its serious consideration. The compromise with family-based child support will at the most yield state provision for the economic support of children who lack complete families at a level somewhere between subsistence and that of the average two-parent family. This is what the Finer Committee recommended and is the result in New Zealand.[33]

III. The Private Obligation

In the United Kingdom, however, for the present, state provision for children of families broken otherwise than by death forms part of state policy towards the poor. At this level a primary right of support is given against the state. The state, in its turn, has, and may exercise, a right to call for contributions by the absent parent. If a child is to seek support above this level, primary recourse must be made against the family's resources. It is therefore necessary to consider the principles upon which such resources should be allocated. We can distinguish two contrasting approaches to determining such allocation: cost sharing and resource sharing.[34] In the first, an attempt is made to calculate the costs of bringing up each child and then to apportion them between the parents. In the second, the resources available to both parents are assessed and an apportionment made between them.

The practice of English courts, so far as can be ascertained, appears to vary between the two approaches. The conventional method of awarding maintenance, whereby a 'child element' is added to a sum awarded in favour of an adult claimant, appears to be directed at meeting the costs, or part thereof, of bringing up the child from the resources of the payer. In *Northrop* v. *Northrop*[35] Diplock LJ said:

> The child must be clothed, housed and tended by the wife. This will involve her in direct expense for food and clothing, etc., for the child. It may involve her indirectly in additional expense for more costly accommodation than would be adequate for herself if living along. It may also involve her in loss of earnings in so far as her ability to undertake paid employment is restricted by the child's needs for her personal care. Provision for the husband to pay or to contribute to these expenses of the wife and to recoup her in whole or in part for her lost earnings may be made by ordering payment of a weekly sum (representing the child element of her maintenance).

He added that as the wife was under a concurrent duty to support the child as well, the courts should consider what her means were, and, if they exceeded what she needed for her own reasonable maintenance, notionally attribute them to the expenses of the child by reducing the husband's liability accordingly. It is, however, rare to find a court making explicit calculations of the kind envisaged in Diplock LJ's judgment. In a survey of the practice of divorce registrars carried out in the early 1970s,[36] no registrar is reported as saying that he made such calculations when apportioning the award as between wife and children. Some were inclined to increase the child element on the ground that 'most men will pay more readily for the children' and because there were tax advantages in adopting this approach.[37] Nor does an examination of the reported cases reveal the use of any such methods. The calculation of child maintenance seems to be quite arbitrary. In *Titheradge* v. *Titheradge*,[38] for example, where the wife was on supplementary benefit and the husband earned £9,576 gross per annum (his second wife earning a further £7,000), the magistrates had varied an order to £35 per week for the wife plus £45 for the remaining teenage dependent child. Balcombe J. thought this would be 'disastrous' for the husband and his second family, and would probably result in a drastic change in their life style. He substituted an order of £20 for the wife and £15 for the child. The judge remarked that he could not see how the magistrates had arrived at the sum of £45 for the child. Yet the current rates of payment to foster parents approved by the National Foster-Care Association were then £34.50 (provinces) and £39 (London), clearly closer to the original order than that of the judge.[39] Since the wife was on supplementary benefit, she could make no contribution towards these expenses. Of course the final order could have been expressed in the form of a single award of £35 for the child. At least this would have had a rational basis.

More usually, at least in lower income cases, the courts seek to apportion resources. *Hall* v. *Hall*[40] may serve as a typical case. The judge had ordered the husband to pay £50 per month to the wife, plus £78 each for the two children (£206 altogether). This was upheld on appeal because when the effect of that order was calculated on the incomes of each household, the result was to leave them at a very similar level.[41] Essentially, this approach distributes the resources of the breadwinner which exceed subsistence level equally between the two households. Whether this approach is consistent with the new provision in the Matrimonial and Family Proceedings Act 1984, that 'first consideration' is to be given to the children of the former marriage, is arguable. It is unlikely that this provision will be of any assistance in determining how resources are to be distributed between such households. It has been said that the courts should not make such a distribution if the result will be to bring the payer's family down to subsistence level[42] but in some cases they seem to have done this.[43] The difficulty here is that if the claimant adult is already in receipt of supplementary benefit, maintenance payments by the other will not confer any benefit on the claimant because if received, they will result only in reduction of the benefit. More usually they are paid directly to the state authorities. Therefore the maintenance payment does not in fact achieve a distribution of resources between the two families. It follows that, in such a case, where the payment has no effect on the claimant family's standard of living, the rationale for achieving an 'equivalence' between the families at subsistence level, disappears. In effect, the goals of resource sharing are confused with the separate purposes of collection by the state of a contribution from the liable relative. The implications of this confusion will be explored later.[44]

(a) Cost sharing

How can the costs of bringing up children be calculated? We need first to estimate the expenses necessary to provide a standard of living at some predetermined level. In other words, there must be an income level to which the costs of the child can be related. We can then calculate what that family would need in terms of additional income after the introduction of a child, in order to maintain the same standard of living it enjoyed without the demands which the child makes on its resources.

A fundamental problem is encountered in determining a method of establishing the living standard which is to apply. In the United States, for example, it was found that low income families spent about one-third of their income on food. An 'economy food plan' was then calculated, and a 'poverty level' was accordingly fixed at three times the sum needed to meet the cost of that plan.[45] There is an element of arbitrariness in choosing food costs as the only baseline from which to fix a standard of living. One might choose some other necessary item. The British practice has been to use an estimate of the wider budgetary requirements of working class families.[46] From this baseline it is possible to move to the second step and calculate the additional expenditure needed both to support a child (of a certain age) and to maintain the family's living standard. This can be done by determining, from Family Expenditure Survey data, what proportion of income is actually spent on children. In this way extra income needs can be expressed as a proportion of the family's actual income. This is done in equivalent income scales which can be used to determine the additions to be made to basic scale rates for various classes of dependent.[47] The major strength of this method is that it takes into account economies of scale achieved by sharing certain costs within a single household.

However, it will be apparent that the figure for the cost of a child yielded by this method, being merely a proportion of the predetermined level of income of a two-adult household without children, simply reflects the level at which that original income is set. How far it is in line with economic reality may be open to dispute.[48] In any case, it tends to embody estimates of the minimal standard of living a society is prepared to tolerate for its members, at a given time. It need not do so, of course. The equivalent income scale could be applied to incomes at any level. The National Foster-Care Association, for example, in fixing its recommendations as to what foster allowances should be paid by local authorities to foster parents (which do not include any wage element) has applied equivalent income scales to a sum calculated as the *average* expenditure on children in a two-adult family.[49]

None of these methods of determining the costs of bringing up a child is suitable for application after parental separation. The use of equivalent income scales presupposes a specific family income or expenditure. What is this to be in the case of the separated family? Is it to be the actual income of the caregiving parent? In many cases this will be no more than supplementary benefit level. The contributor's payment (if made in full) would do no more than compensate the state for the child additions to the supplementary benefit payments. The technique would accept the poverty level as the proper one at which the child's living standards are to be set. But this is a very questionable assumption if the contributor is in a financial position to improve that level. Furthermore, as Cassetty[50] points out, this may lead to the notion that such minimal standards are all that is necessary, fair, and reasonable. Similarly, if the caregiver's earnings have raised the level above the poverty line, the restriction of the absent parent's obligation to the equivalent income scale accepts that the basic standard of living of the children is set by the caregiver's earnings. But our data have demonstrated how inadequate these are. A different approach was suggested by Levin (1983),[51] based on the recommended foster allowances. The absent parent is to be considered primarily liable (in so far as his resources permit) to pay a sum equivalent to the recommended foster allowance for a child of the same age, less a deduction of any contribution it is thought should reasonably be made by the caregiving parent. But, as we have seen, the recommended sum *assumes* a family expenditure at the national average. There is some basis for making this assumption in the case of foster families. These are unlikely to be single parent families. They will share many of the characteristics of the 'average' family. They are families into which a foster child has been introduced, with respect to which they can apply economies of scale. But these assumptions cannot be made in the case of single parent families. The figure yielded will bear no relation to that family's standard of living. The economies of scale which produce the sum by the application of equivalence scales in a two-adult, single-earner household do not apply. The earner will have two households to maintain. In relation to the post-divorce situation, the figure is quite arbitrary.

Another way in which equivalence scales might be used in relation to child support would be to apply them in each case to the joint incomes of the adults. The purpose would be to determine the cost of keeping the child at the level it had enjoyed before the divorce. But this too must be rejected, mainly for the same reason as the previous suggestion. The assumption of household unity, on which the scales rest, has collapsed. This will most obviously effect housing costs, one of the most significant economies of scale achieved by the introduction of more persons into the one household.[52] Even if the figure yielded by an application of the equivalence scales to the father's income were paid by some third party to a child and its caregiver living separately from the father, it certainly cannot be assumed that this would maintain that unit at the previous level.

We conclude that the traditional methods of costing child upbringing can be of no useful application in establishing norms for determining the appropriate level of child support after divorce. The fundamental reason for this is that the amount which people spend on their children depends on the income they have.[53] If their income is very low, it is possible to introduce concepts of minimal living standards, including child maintenance, but these are inappropriate to determining the support obligation across families. The cost of a child can, therefore, only be assessed in relation to the standard of living of its family. But our problem is to know how to settle that standard of living. Is it to be that of the caregiver and child? Or that of the absent parent? Or is some amalgam to be constructed? Only by using a resource-sharing approach can these issues be properly confronted.

(b) Resource sharing

Isabel Sawhill[54] has set out a basic model for the sharing of resources for child support. It is based on two principles. First, that after divorce children should be supported at a level commensurate with their standard of living before divorce, if consistent with the second principle: that where a reduction in standards of living is required because two households must now be supported instead of one, there should be equal sharing of available resources between the two households after adjustments for differences in family size.

If we adopt this approach, it is necessary to apportion the actual incomes of the adults in some way between the families. An equal split will not suffice for it will fail to recognize the new basis upon which economies of scale operate after separation. For the economies which applied when the family was together have been replaced by circumstances where they operate only for the unit comprising the caregiver and the children. It is therefore appropriate to use figures derived from equivalent income scales to take this factor into account (Table 7.1). If we take the equivalent of a single, adult householder as being 0.61 and of children aged three and six as being 0.18 and 0.21 respectively,[56] and apply this to a broken family with children of those ages living with a sole adult caregiver, when the combined incomes of the adults amount to £12,000, it is apparent that for the caregiver and children to maintain the same standard of living after the separation as they enjoyed before, it is necessary to calculate 61 per cent of £12,000 (£7,320) and add to that (0.18 + 0.21) per cent of £7,320 (£2,855), giving a total of £10,175. This would leave a mere £1,825 in the hands of the absent parent. This

Table 7.1. *Equivalence scales calculated by the Economic Advisor's Office (DHSS) compared with supplementary benefit relativities**

	EAO equivalent income scale[†]		Ordinary SB scale-rate relativities[‡]
	Including housing costs	Excluding housing costs	
Household type:			
Married couple, wife not working	1.00	1.00	1.00
Single adult, householder	0.61	0.55	0.61
2nd adult, non-householder	0.46	0.45	⎫
3rd adult, non-householder	0.42	0.45	⎬ 0.49
4th adult, non-householder	0.36	0.40	⎭
Child aged:			
0–1	0.09	0.07	⎫ 0.18
2–4	0.18	0.18	⎭
5–7	0.21	0.21	⎫ 0.21
8–10	0.23	0.23	⎭
11–12	0.25	0.26	0.26
13–15	0.27	0.28	0.32
16–18	0.36	0.38	0.38

* Taken from R. van Slooten and A. G. Coverdale (1978).[55]
† Average of scales calculated from 1971 and 1972 FES data for United Kingdom.
‡ This scale applies to 1971 and also to 1972.

calculation demonstrates the impossibility of Sawhill's first principle, and the inevitability of its qualification by the second.

It is possible, however, as Sawhill demonstrates, to build the second principle into the calculation. An equivalence scale can indicate how much income a mother living alone with children needs to maintain a living standard equivalent to that of any given individual. The caregiving parent's share of the combined income would not be equal to that of the absent parent, but would be increased by the proportion which she would need to maintain equivalence with him. Thus, to revert to our example, the equivalence scales show that two children aged three and six require a 39 per cent increase in family income if the family is to maintain its living standard. This would be added to the caregiving parent's share in dividing the combined income. The absent parent's share would be determined thus: (*a*) £12,000/(1 + 1.39) = £5,020. This leaves the caregiving parent with £12,000 − £5020 = £6980.[7]

Such a formula, which we call the 'equalization formula', merely gives a basis upon which further adjustments can be made. Sawhill, for example, would increase the caregiving parent's share by throwing on the absent parent part of the child care expenses which the caregiving parent would be assumed incur while she was earning part of the combined income. Important adjustments would occur if there is a distribution of children between the adults. If there is to be equality between the children, the weightings would need to reflect the distribution. Thus, if one parent looked after two children of three and six and the other cared for a child under two, the formula determining the distribution ratio would read: (*b*) £12,000 = £5,286 (1 + 1.39)/1.09 The parent with the infant would receive £5,286 and the other, £6,714.

If, however, the absent parent reconstitutes his family and his household consists of another adult and a child under two, a further reduction in the amount the original caregiver would receive must be made according to the formula: (*c*) £12,000 = £6,185 (1 + 1.39)/1.48*

The maintenance payer can now keep £6,185 of the £12,000 on account of the needs of his new household, leaving the other household with £5,815. We may illustrate the distribution of income in these different cases in tabular form, assuming the absent parent to be the man (Table 7.2.).

Principles need to be developed to settle the sum which has been described above as the 'combined' income of the adults. If the caregiving

---

* This figure is derived from Table 7.1 and assumes that an increase in income of 0.09 per cent for a child under two and 0.39 per cent for the other adult is necessary to maintain the absent parent's standard of living.

Table 7.2. *Distribution of joint income of £12,000, maintaining equivalence in living standard*

	Man	Woman with two children aged three and six
Man living alone	5,020	6,980
Man living with one child under two	5,286	6,714
Man living with new partner and child under two	6,185	5,815

adult was earning, the resultant maintenance obligation would prima facie be no more than what was necessary to make up the difference (if any) between that earned income and the sum awardable to the caregiver's family under the above formulae, with possible additions for child care expenses incurred by the caregiver's employment. If the caregiver was not earning, it would need to be decided whether it would be reasonable to expect this and, accordingly, whether a deduction should be made for notional earnings. Another difficult question would be whether the maintenance obligation should be based upon earnings at the time of divorce or should reflect subsequent changes in standards of living. This question will be dealt with in our discussion on upper and lower limits, in the next section. A related question is whether contributions to the household income by a new partner should be included in the calculation of the combined income. The answer to this question, of course, presupposes that post-divorce changes in income can be taken into account; it too will be discussed in the next section.

(c) Upper limits: the concept of the normative standard

It is manifest that the adoption of the principles discussed in the previous section run counter to the tide of recent developments in maintenance law, which is to abolish, or severely limit, the persistence of a post-divorce maintenance obligation. For under these formulae the absent parent will need to share his resources in such a way as to keep the children *and former spouse* as nearly as can be at a standard of living equivalent to that which they enjoyed at the time of separation. On the view we take of equity to children, we believe this approach to be in principle correct. However, the extent of its application justifies closer scrutiny. Does it, for example, require that the wife and children of a very wealthy individual should be maintained at a very high standard during the dependency of the children? Would it require that the wife and children should be entitled to share in all the wealth a man might acquire after divorce? We believe that we can sensibly construct upper limits to the application of this principle, partly out of further considerations of principle, and partly out of recognition that some compromise with the competing claims of the potential payer to the free use of his resources, and their further commitment to a second family, may be required in order to make our principle more easily acceptable.

We need at this point to reconsider the arguments for state intervention at all on the breakdown of marriage. Primarily, as we have seen, community concern arises from the fact that the normal social mechanism (the family) of ensuring an adequate standard of living for the children, has failed. As against most (though not all) other children in the community, these children are disadvantaged. We have reviewed the evidence which suggests that this disadvantage may have long-term implications for the realization by these children of their life chances. In principle, the state should step in to make good this deficiency. The community should ensure that these children at least enjoy the standard of living of the child in the average two-parent family. But, as we have seen, the political constraints against such a degree of state provision are presently too great. The fundamental conception upon which our approach to the private law child-support obligation rests is that it represents the *diversion through state machinery, of private resources, to satisfy the children's claims against the community*. If these fall short, public provision continues to provide a safety net. This claim is distinct from any other that might be grounded in express or implied undertakings by one party to the other, or the satisfaction of expectations reasonably held in a particular family context. We do not totally exclude the relevance of claims so based to child support or post-divorce maintenance generally, but believe that their scope is limited in practice and should be severely circumscribed in principle. We do not see as compelling an argument that (whatever morality may say) legal means should be available to the children of the rich to ensure that their father keeps them at his own indulgent standards, even after marriage breakdown. We can certainly argue that they should not thereby be rendered worse off than the children of the average, intact family. But should their position of advantage be legally underwritten?

We are prepared to introduce a significant qualification to the principle of equalization of resources, by the introduction of an upper limit to the child-support obligation set at a standard of living which we shall call the 'normative standard'. This is designed to encompass the principle that, if available resources can prevent it, children should not fall below, or further below than can be avoided, a standard of living enjoyed by most children in their society. The concept goes beyond the ideal of 'belonging' to, or 'participation' in a community which is employed in the poverty literature.[58] The children should not merely be entitled to feel that they are part of the community of intact families, but that they are a *standard case* of that community. The major determinant of this standard will be set by the family's income, as related to its household composition. Whether the appropriate standard is found by reference to the modal level of earnings (the level received by a larger number of earnings than any other), the median level (that at which half earners earn less and the other half earn more), or to some other referrant, is a technical matter beyond our immediate concern. The standard, thus set, would be applied to each particular case by means of equivalence scales. The result would be the normative standard as we conceive it and would be the ruling standard by which child support awards should be set, and which would in time become accepted as the societal norm in this matter.

As our data demonstrate, the level of child support set in this way would require higher payments than are presently made in the vast majority of cases. If the payer's means are inadequate, then, subject to the application of a lower limit, which we shall discuss shortly, the equalization principle requires the extent of the shortfall to be shared between the parties. The question arises whether the normative standard should be capable of being overridden in the relatively few cases where private resources permit this. We do not view our standard as a device for imposing *undue* inflexibility, but its significant advantages, which we detail below, would be lost unless it could be disregarded only in exceptional cases. In two respects, however, the concept would need to be modified. We cannot totally exclude reference to the possibly adverse consequences of change in itself on the life chances of the children of divorce. In this respect, a change from private-to public-sector education, or from private- to public-sector housing, might result in additional disadvantage for individual children even though family income was kept to the norm. The solution in such cases is to build into the norm, as applied to the specific family, a housing and education factor which would seek to retain the children, so far as possible, if not at a particular address or institution, at least within the sector to which they are accustomed.

The major gain to be achieved by establishing a normative standard would be the reorientation of the theoretical basis of post-divorce support from one grounded essentially in private undertakings to a community based obligation. But there are also powerful practical arguments. A clearly defined standard would provide a yardstick around which negotiations for out-of-court settlements could take place. The scope for variation according to subjective judicial discretion would be greatly reduced. Perhaps more importantly, if there were no limit to the extent of the obligation, the payer would remain under continued threat of a significant drain on resources acquired after divorce, with corresponding ill effects on incentives and profits for his new family. The limit also offers protection for resources brought into any new family he may form with a new partner. It would seem axiomatic that the maintenance obligation which falls on the payer should not exceed the resources he himself generates. So if, for example, his obligation is assessed at £5,000 but he brings in no income, he should pay nothing even if his new partner earns £10,000 (unless the whole arrangement is contrived). But if, in such a case, he and his partner each earns £5,000, should the full £5,000 be exacted against the man on the ground that his household is still left with £5,000? In principle, we believe it should, but only so far as it would bring his former family up to the standard of the norm. It is indisputable that the man's living standards are partially determined by his partner's income. If his standard is thereby raised up to, or above, the norm, it is difficult to see why the element which he contributes to it should not be available to push his former family as near as possible to that standard. But once it has reached that level, income from his new partner, like increases in his own post-divorce income, should accrue solely to the benefit of his new family.

On this basis, the final calculation of the proportion of the joint income to which the caregiving parent would be entitled would require an initial calculation of that family's supplementary benefit entitlement, the application of the appropriate multiplier to determine what would need to be that family's income to bring it up to the norm level and, if the resulting figure was lower than the proportion allocated to that family by the formulae used in the preceding section, to deduct that sum from the maintenance payable. (See Example (a)). In this example, the norm is assumed to be set at 200 per cent of the family's supplementary benefit entitlement.)

Example (a)
Man earning £9,000   Woman earning £3,000
Combined income = £12,000

> After divorce, man living alone, woman living with children aged three and six.
> Distribution according to equivalence formula: Man = £5,020; Woman = £6,980.
> Norm income for caregiving family = £5,000 (i.e. 200 per cent of their supplementary benefit entitlement)
> Maintenance obligation: (£6,980 − £3,000) − (£6,980 − £5,000) = £2,000.

If the allocation of resources between the adults yields insufficient to bring the caregiving family up to norm income levels, the support obligation will prima facie need to be paid in full. The operation of the principle of equality may be to bring the payer, and his new family if he has one, below the norm level too. It may be argued that the norm income level should act as a lower limit below which the payer's standard of living should not be allowed to fall. For if it does, two sets of children (if he has children) would be suffering disadvantage rather than one.[59] Our data have shown that 50 per cent of men paying maintenance have household income above supplementary benefit level but below the average. If such payers were to be excluded, there would be a sharp fall in the extent of child support paid. We are not convinced that such an exclusion would be justified. We therefore believe that the equality principle should apply at this level of income as well. However, this is subject to an important qualification.

(d) Lower limits: the supplementary benefit formula

Many of the child support payments made by people of below average incomes are effectively payments to the state, for they simply offset the level of supplementary benefit payable to the caregiver. In that event, the reduction in the payer's living standard does not enure to the benefit of the caregiver. The use of the equalization formula is frustrated, for the money thereby drawn off from the absent parent does not go towards equalizing the standard of living of the two families, but simply reduces the standard of the absent parent, to the benefit of none but the state. We have argued earlier that the purposes (and therefore the method) of extracting money from a liable relative are different from the enforcement of a support obligation between families. Whether the state should reduce families below the average, or some other level, in its recoupment exercise, is another question. For that reason, the authorities collecting contributions from 'liable relatives' have used a formula which permits the liable persons to retain a proportion of their income representing their supplementary entitlement (plus rent) and, additionally, one quarter of their net income.[60] The courts, however, seeing their role as equalizing the income between the parties, or, sometimes, as guardians of the ethos of family responsibility, have ignored the formula, even if the whole or major part of the support payment would pass to the state,[1] effectively overriding the exclusion of former spouses from the class of liable relatives under social security law.[61]

The dilemma at the lower end of the income scales is whether the equalization formula should be applied when its application would leave the maintenance payer with a final income lower than that which he would be allowed to keep if the caregiving parent were wholly supported by supplementary benefit and the state simply sought contribution from him. There are strong reasons for abandoning the equalization formula in this situation. One is that not to do so would lead to anomalies between different maintenance payers, as the following examples show. In the ensuing discussion these abbreviations are used

WSBL = Wife's supplementary-benefit level
HSBL = Husband's supplementary-benefit level
HI   = Husband's income
HSBF = Income that husband should retain on supplementary benefit formula
EF   = Equalization formula
CS   = Child-support (amount)
HFI   = Husband's final income
WFI   = Wife's final income
AHFI = Husband's final income after adjustment
ACS   = Adjusted child-support payment
AWFI = Wife's final income after adjustment

Example (b) low income earner

HI = £48   WSBL = £30
HSBL = £22   (W living alone
                                            with children aged
                                            three and six)

HSBF = £22 + £48 = £34
EF = HFI £48/ (1 + 1.39) = £20.80
CS = £48 − £20.80 = £27.20 = WFI

$$CS < WSBL \text{ therefore } AHFI = HSBF$$
$$= £34$$
$$AWFI = WSBL$$
$$= £30.$$

H contributes $HI - HSBF = £14$ to the state.

Example (c) Average-income earner

HI = £62	WSBL = £30
HSBL = £22	(W living alone with children aged three and six)

$$HSBF = £22 + £62/4 = £37.50$$
$$EF = HFI = £62/(1 + 1.39) = £25.90$$
$$CS = £62 - £25.90 = £36.10 = WFI.$$

In example (b), the amount of child support payable under the equalization formula is less than the sum the wife would receive in supplementary benefit. Since the husband is unable, on this formula, to raise his wife and children above supplementary benefit level, the wife will remain at that level and his payment will partially offset the state benefit. But, since this is no more than an excise of the state's right of recourse, the state will not bring his income below that set by the supplementary benefit formula (£34, in our example). In the second case, however (which is closely modelled on the facts of *Shallow* v. *Shallow*[62]), the husband is a higher earner. He is therefore able (on the equalization formula) to raise his wife above supplementary benefit level. But this can only be done by reducing him well below the level which would have been permitted under the supplementary benefit formula. In fact, his final income would be *lower* than that of the lower earning husband of Example (b). Although the final figures are a little different (because the court did not use the equalization formula), this was essentially the result of the decision in *Shallow* v. *Shallow*. But the result must be unacceptable as creating severe inequity between the two classes of payer, brought about by their differences in income or the chance that private maintenance proceedings had been brought in one case but not the other. A further objection to ignoring the supplementary benefit formula is that, without using some formula such as this, the payer's final income might be set so low that he would lose an incentive to work. This difficulty was brushed aside in *Shallow* v. *Shallow*, where Ormrod LJ said, 'the probability of the husband giving up his job and a net income (after payment of the amount due under the order) of about £31 per week for supplementary benefit at a rate of £22 per week seems remote'. But this observation ignores the expenses associated with employment (transport, meals, clothing) and hidden advantages of supplementary benefit which can act as a passport to other benefits. It would seem desirable to maintain a single criterion which can include an element related to the maintenance of work incentives.

Another objection to proceeding as illustrated in Example (c) is that in that case the state makes an unwarranted gain. For, in Example (b), the net outlay of the state to the wife was WSBL − (HI − HSBF) or £30 − £14 = £16. In the second case, because the husband was brought below the level set by the supplementary benefit formula, the state outlay to the wife was £0. There seems little reason why the state should relieve the first couple of that degree of expenditure, but make no contribution in the second case. One way partially to redress this imbalance is to calculate the sum which the state would have borne if, in Example (b), the husband had been unable, under the equalization formula, to raise the wife above supplementary benefit level, according to the formula WSBL − (HI − HSBF). In our case this is £30 − (£62 − £37.50) = £5.50. This sum represents the gain to the state brought about by the reduction of the husband's income below the level of the supplementary benefit formula. The state should therefore pay this sum to the wife, who would take it in addition to child support, and reduce the husband's child-support liability by the same amount, yielding the following conclusion (the 'adjustment formula'):

ACS = CS − £5.50 = £30.60
AHFI = HI(£62) − ACS (£30.60) = £31.40
AWFI = ACS (£30.60) + £5.50 = £36.10.

The wife ends up with the sum allocated to her under the equalization formula and the husband is somewhat better off than he would have been without the adjustment. His final income position, however, still falls short of the husband in Example (b).

(e) A disregard?

However, if, in a case like Example (c), the supplementary benefit formula were maintained, the husband would be left with an income of

£37.50 and the wife would stay at supplementary benefit level of £30. The wife's income stands at a proportion of 0.8 of that of the husband, whereas under the equalization formula it should stand at 1.4. This is a serious departure from the equalization norm and very detrimental to the caregiver and the children. (Under the adjustment formula the proportion is 1.14.) We would therefore argue that, as a minimal measure, a procedure such as the adjustment suggested here should be adopted, where the payer is able to pay sufficient child support to take the caregiver off supplementary benefit level but where he, in turn,would thereby be reduced below the level set by the supplementary benefit formula. This would reduce the child support he would be required to pay without detriment to the caregiver.

We would, however, prefer another solution to the problem. We believe that the objections to using the equalization formula so as to override the supplementary benefit formula are sufficiently compelling that the latter should always form a bottom limit to the amount of child support which an absent parent should be ordered to pay. However, at present this concession accrues entirely to the benefit of that individual. In most cases, to apply this limit would leave the caregiver and the children at supplementary benefit level. The only way in which this can be overcome is by introducing a disregard which would allow the recipient to bolster her family income by adding an element of maintenance payment to supplementary benefit.

There are strong parallel arguments for adopting this course. We have shown, in our data, how frequently support payments are made, how (though small in themselves) they may constitute a not insignificant contribution to the recipient family's resources, but how frequently they merely disappear into the state treasury. The extent to which child-support payments, in some form or another are made, suggests how widespread is the ethic that an absent parent should support his children. At low income levels, if such an ethos is to survive, the payers must be offered some incentive. This can only be found in the conferment of some visible benefit on the children. On broader policy grounds, we can argue that, in the case of these children, there exist some resources which may not be available to others, but which can be used to reduce (if not in most cases to remove totally) the relative deprivation caused by divorce. We might also cite in support the introduction of a disregard for child support payments made to welfare (AFDC) recipients introduced in the United States in 1984.

The disregard would, therefore, apply in all cases where the payment made by the absent parent failed to lift the caregiver above supplementary benefit level. How might the level of disregard be fixed? This might be done on a universal basis, applying the same disregard in all cases. It might, on the other hand, be calculated on a case by case basis so as to bear some relation to the amount of child support actually paid. One principled way of doing this is to calculate the advantage which the state confers on the payer by permitting him to retain income at the supplementary-benefit-formula level. It could be argued that the proportion by which that level exceeds his supplementary benefit entitlement should equally be applied in the case of the wife, so that she should be permitted to retain any child support payments which would have the effect of raising her final income above supplementary benefit level by the same proportion. So if the supplementary benefit formula leaves the payer with, say, 170 per cent of his supplementary benefit entitlement, the caregiver prima facie should be entitled to retain support payments sufficient to bring her up to 170 per cent above her supplementary benefit level. The disregard (D) is thus calculated by the following formula:

$$D = \frac{WSBL}{HSBL/(HSBF-HSBL)}$$

In Example (b) the disregard would be £10, and in Example (c) it would be £21.40. While in principle the caregiver should be entitled to 100 per cent of the disregard figure, public expenditure considerations might reduce the proportion which would be allowed. The net result in a case like *Shallow* v. *Shallow* (Example (c)) would be that the husband's income would remain at supplementary benefit formula level (£37.50), the wife's final income would be £41.40, and the husband would pay £24.50 child support, of which the state would receive only £3.10. The state would be the net loser by (£30 − £3.10) = £26.90, because under the actual decision, no supplementary benefit would have been payable to the wife since the court ignored the floor to child support payments created by the supplementary benefit formula.

It should be stressed that in cases where a lower limit to child support applied, the resulting income position between the parties would not bear any necessary relation to that which would be indicated by the equalization formula. The purpose of the disregard is not primarily to reintroduce an element of equalization between the distribution of resources of the individuals (though it does go some way towards this), but to equalize *the state*'s contribution to broken families at low incomes. For as it presently operates, the application of the supplementary benefit formula benefits only one party to the maintenance equation, and applies unevenly among payers. It follows that the introduction of any disregard cannot effect cases of higher income earners where a distribution of income, even when subjected to the lower limit, provides sufficient funds for the caregiving parent to raise her above supplementary benefit level. This is illustrated in Example (d):

Example (d)

HI	$= £80$	WSBL $= £30$
HSB	$= £22$	
HSBF	$= £22 + £80/4 = £42$	
EF	$= \text{HFI} = £80/(1 + 1.39) = £33.50$	
	CS $= £80 - £33.50 = £46.50$	
	$= \text{WFI}$	
	HFI $(£33.50) < \text{HSBF} (£42)$.	

Therefore:

AHFI	$= £42$
ACS	$= £80 - £42 = £38 \ (= \text{AWFI})$.

The wife, in this situation, ends up with £38, rather than £46.50 as indicated by the equalization formula. But since that sum is in excess of her supplementary benefit level, there is no room for the operation of a disregard. The conclusion is an inevitable consequence of the distortion of the equalization formula caused by acceptance of a lower limit on child-support payments. But, unless the state is prepared to step in with a class of excess payments in order to redress this inequality, the result is unavoidable. In an area where uncomfortable compromises are necessary, we would prefer to maintain a uniform lower limit for child-support payments and permit a series of disregards to alleviate the situation of the worst-off families.

The preceding discussion of a possible role for a disregard is, of course, located within the context of the present system of state support. But the employment of a disregard might also be important even on the hypothesis that the state was prepared on its own account to provide a guaranteed income to children of broken families. For reasons given earlier in this chapter, it seems unlikely that the level of such provision would be equivalent to the average income of a two-parent family. If the state were to have recourse against the absent parent, it would seem important that this should not be treated only as an exercise in revenue collection. Some, at any rate, of the money raised from that parent should be permitted to supplement the household income of the single parent family, at least until it reaches the level of the 'normative standard' expounded earlier. In this way a rational and coherent balance might be achieved between the roles of public and private law in the area of child support.

(f) Other adjustments

(i) Wife's earnings

The above discussion has, for convenience, proceeded on the assumption that the wife has no earned income of her own. If she has such income, it will be introduced into the equations by adding it to that of the husband. Example (b) therefore would be resolved as follows, if the wife has sufficient earnings to keep her clear of reliance on supplementary benefit (WE denotes the wife's earnings):

Example (e)

$$
\begin{aligned}
\text{HI} \quad &= \pounds62 \qquad\qquad \text{WE} = \pounds40 \\
\text{HSB} \quad &= \pounds22 \\
\text{HSBF} \quad &= \pounds22 + \pounds62/4 = \pounds37.50 \\
\text{EF:} \quad &\text{HFI} = (\text{HI} + \text{WE})/(1 + 1.39) = \pounds42.60 \\
&\text{CS} = [(\text{HI} + \text{WE}) - \pounds42.60 \\
&\quad\ = (\pounds102 - \pounds42.6) - \pounds40 \\
&\quad\ = \pounds19.40 \\
&\text{WFI} = \text{CS} + \text{WE} = \pounds59.40.
\end{aligned}
$$

Example (e) is straightforward in so far as HFI exceeds HSBF and there is no supplementary benefit element in the wife's income. We may, however, consider the situation where neither of those propositions is true. Suppose the wife has part-time earnings of £20. If her normal supplementary benefit entitlement is £30, she will be left with a total income of £42 on account of the maximum disregard of £12 permitted for part-time earnings in the case of a single parent, of which £20 will represent her earnings and £22 supplementary benefit. In applying the equalization formula, the supplementary benefit element should be omitted from the initial equation (Example (f)).

Example (f)

HFI = £62 + £20/4 = £34.30
HFI (£34.30) < HSBF (£37.50).

Therefore
CS = HI − HSBF = £24.50
WFI = WI + CS = £44.50.

Since the wife's earnings (£20) and the child support lift the wife clear of the level she would have been at had she remained on supplementary benefit (£44.50 as opposed to £42), no question of disregard arises. The husband is left with an income of £37.50 and he pays the wife £24.50 in child support. But the husband may be poorer, as in Example (g) so that the disregard comes into play.

Example (g)

HI = £44	WSBL = £30
HSBL = £22	WE = £20
HSBF = £22 + £44/4 = £33	WSB = (£30 + £12) − £20
	= £22
	Wife's total income (WTI) = £42

EF: HFI = (£44 + £20)/(1 + 1.39) = £26.70
HFI (£26.7) < HSBF (£33).

Therefore:
CS = HI − HSBF = £11
WFI = WE + CS = £33
WFI = £42.

Therefore apply disregard:

$$\frac{\text{WSBL (£30)}}{\text{HSBL (£22)/[HSBF(£33) −HSBL(£22)]}} = £30/2 = £15.$$

It is arguable that this disregard of £15 should apply both to the wife's earnings and the child-support payment. For that represents an excess above her supplementary benefit entitlement comparable to that permitted to her husband, and there is no reason why child support should take her above that level. On this view, since £12 of the £15 represents the disregard attributable to her earnings, she can add a further £3 from the child support. The final position therefore would be that the husband has £33, the wife £45, and the state recovers (£11−£3) = £8 from the husband. The disregard would never, of course, be less than the £12 allowed for part-time earnings.

(ii) Husband's new commitments

The examples discussed so far have assumed the husband to be a single man, with no dependants. The introduction of dependants will, of course, entail important modifications to the calculations. In Example (h) it is assumed that he has remarried a woman with a child aged five:

Example (h)

HI = £62   WSBL = £30

    Equivalence scale for wife and child aged 5 =

    (0.39 + 0.21) = 0.60

    HSBL = £40

    HSBF = £40 + £62/4 = £55.50.

    EF: HFI = £62/(1 + 1.39/1.60) = £33.30

            HFI < HSBF

            CS = £62 − £55.50 = £6.50

            CS < WSBL.

            Therefore apply disregard

$$D = \frac{£30}{£40/(£55.50 - £40)} = £11.50$$

The disregard being higher than the child support, the total child support should be disregarded, leaving the husband with a final income of £55.50, the wife with £36.50, and the state's position unchanged.

(iii) Housing costs and capital transfers

Since it is evident that housing costs form a significant element in determining an individual's and a family's standard of living, such costs must be included in these calculations. The total child support sum should comprise all elements in the payments made by the absent parent which are directed at housing costs. If property transfer has taken place, its equivalent value in terms of income should be determined and considered a constituent element of child support payments. The same should be done with respect to other forms of capital transfer. The desirability of modifying (or expanding) the concept of the normative standard in order to retain a child in private sector housing was discussed above (see p. 122).

(iv) Other adjustments

In assessing the incomes of the parties which are to be treated as the net incomes for the purposes of the relevant calculations, it would be proper, in appropriate circumstances, to make various adjustments. For example, a fixed sum which a person has to pay in support of some other person, perhaps an elderly relative[62] or even other dependents living outside his household, should be deducted. Such sums do not properly constitute part of the income available either for equalization purposes or recourse by the state. A special rule as regards education was suggested in our discussion of the concept of the normative standard (see p. 122).

Notes

1. See *Robinson* v. *Robinson* [1983] Fam. 42; *Ibbetson* v. *Ibbetson* (1984) 14 Family Law 309. Contrast *Vasay* v. *Vasay* (1984) The Times 13 November.
2. *Murcutt* v. *Murcutt* [1953] P. 266.
3. See John Eekelaar (1979), 'Some Principles of Financial and Property Adjustment on Divorce', 95 *Law Quarterly Rev.*, pp. 253–67.
4. For similar arguments, see I. Sawhill (1983), 'Developing Normative Standards for Child-Support Payments', in Judith Cassetty (ed.), *The Parental Child-Support Obligation* (Lexington Mass., Lexington Books), p. 82; Carol Bruch (1983), 'Child Support Payments: A Critique', op. cit. p. 124; see also Leslie McClements (1978), *The Economics of Social Security* (London, Heinemann), pp. 99–101, on the effects of joint consumption and economies of scale in households.
5. See above p. 12.
6. i.e. the parents.
7. Matrimonial Causes Act 1973, s. 25 (2). The obligation is qualified by reference to the parents' circumstances and other responsibilities.
8. See above, Chapter 2.
9. Law Commission (1969), *Financial Provision in Matrimonial Proceedings*, Law Com. No. 25, Explanatory Note to clause 5 of the Draft Bill, para. 3.
10. Matrimonial and Family Proceedings Act 1984, s. 3.
11. See above, p. 15.
12. See Kevin Gray (1977), *The Reallocation of Property on Divorce* (Abingdon, Professional Books); Law Commission (1981), *The Financial Consequences of Divorce*, Law Com. No. 112, para. 17; 445 HL Deb. col. 37 (Lord Hailsham); col. 57 (Lord Denning).
13. See Edward M. Young (1983), 'Threshold Issues Associated with the Parental Obligation of Child Support', in Cassetty (1983), ch. 5.

14. Margaret Wynn (1972), *Family Policy* (London, Michael Joseph).
15. See Hilary Land (1975), 'The Introduction of Family Allowances: An Act of Historical Justice?', in Hall *et al.*, *Change, Choice and Conflict in Social Policy* (London, Heinemann).
16. See the criticisms of the practice of the Supplementary Benefits Commission in the *Report of the Committee on One-Parent Families* (Finer Report) (1974), Cmnd. 5629, vol. 1, paras. 4.199–202. Similar practices were followed in Australia (*Report of the Joint Select Committee on the Family Law Act* (1980), vol. 1, para. 5.29) and New Zealand (*Report of The Royal Commission of Inquiry: Social Security in New Zealand* (1972), ch. 35, para. 5).
17. See the discussion in Mary Ann Glendon (1981), *The New Family and the New Property* (Toronto, Butterworth), pp. 72–6.
18. See A. Agell (1979), 'Social Security and Family Law in Sweden', in A. Samuels (ed.), *Social Security and Family Law* (UK Comparative Law Series No. 4).
19. John Eekelaar (1984), *Family Law and Social Policy* (London, Weidenfeld and Nicolson), pp. 123–5.
20. HC Deb. vol. 898, col. 62 (20 Oct. 1975).
21. Finer Report (1974), vol. 1, para. 5.112.
22. Ibid. para. 5.106.
23. Ibid. para. 5.106.
24. Below, p. 122.
25. Social Security Amendment Act 1973; [1975] *New Zealand . Law Journal*, p. 6.
26. Social Security Amendment Act 1980.
27. W. R. Atkin (1981), 'Liable Relatives: The New State Role in Ordering Maintenance', 5 *Otago Law Rev.*, 48.
28. Atkin (1981), 48, at p. 63.
29. Only in 1948 did grandparents cease to be 'liable relatives' in English law.
30. See the remarks of Ormrod LJ in *Tovey* v. *Tovey* (1978) 8 Family Law 80: 'it was very undesirable indeed that a man should not, even in a purely formal sense, continue to contribute to the children who were his primary liability . . . certainly as a matter of principle it must be right that a man should regard his own children as his primary obligation. If that position was abandoned, it became a very disorderly and disorganized situation'. See also *Freeman* v. *Swatridge* (1984) 14 Family Law 215.
31. See Mary Hayes (1983), 'Maintenance Defaulters – Are Poor Men Wrongfully sent to prison?', 13 *Family Law*, pp. 243–8, and above p. 30.
32. See A. Cherlin (1981), *Marriage, Divorce, Remarriage* (Cambridge, Harvard University Press), p. 136 n. 31, for the American literature.
33. The Finer Committee rejected suggestions that provision for one-parent families should be analogous to the allowance paid to widowed mothers. Their reasons were (i) that allowance is payable regardless of other income sources; (ii) in widowhood there is no other source of family income, whereas other single-parent families may have recourse against a separated father; (iii) it could not equitably be paid to lone fathers who were in employment, regardless of their income; (iv) the level of the benefit would still leave many families at subsistence level; (v) the new benefit would in any case have to be administered separately from widows' benefits (Finer Report (1974), vol. 1, para. 5.102). But it is possible to take all these objections into

account (as does the New Zealand system) while taking the level of the widows' benefit as the referent for the single-parent family's benefit.

34. See generally Judith Cassetty, 'Emerging Issues in Child-Support Policy and Practice', in Cassetty (1983) ch. 1.

35. [1967] 2 All ER 961 at p. 979.

36. W. Barrington Baker *et al.* (1977), *The Matrimonial Jurisdiction of Registrars* (Oxford, SSRC Centre for Socio-Legal Studies), para. 3.6.

37. See above, p. 26.

38. (1983) 13 Family Law 83; Reference may also be made to *Watchel* v. *Watchel* [1973] Fam. 72; *Hector* v. *Hector* [1973] 3 All ER 1070;*Poulter* v. *Poulter* (1974) 4 Family Law, 86; *Strelley-Upton* v. *Strelley-Upton* (1974) 4 Family Law 9 (£12 per week for wife and £2.50 each for children of 16 and 14); *Harnett* v. *Harnett* [1973] Fam. 156 (child element increased from £4 to £10 without reasons); *Lewis* v. *Lewis* [1977] 3 All ER 992; *Scott* v. *Scott* [1978] 3 All ER 65 (decisions made by comparing standards of living of respective groups); *Camm* v. *Camm* (1983) 13 Family Law 112 (lack of distinction between child and adult elements).

39. See Editorial Note (1983) 13 Family Law, 84.

40. (1984) 14 Family Law 54.

41. See also, the cases cited in Chapter 3, n. 107.

42. *Roberts* v. *Roberts* [1970] P. 1.

43. *Tovey* v. *Tovey* (1978) 8 Family Law 80; *Girvan* v. *Girvan* (1983) 13 Family Law 213.

44. See below, pp. 125–7.

45. US Department of Health Education and Welfare (1976), *Income Supplement Program*: *1974 HEW Welfare Replacement Proposal*, Technical Analysis Paper 11 (Office of Income Security Policy, Washington, DC).

46. McClements (1978), pp. 52–3.

47. R. van Slooten and A. G. Coverdale (1978), 'The Characteristics of Low Income Households', *Social Trends*, No. 8 (London, HMSO), p. 8.

48. See the criticisms of the British supplementary benefit scale-rates, by David Piachaud (1979), *The Cost of a Child: A Modern Minimum* (London, Child Poverty Action Group) and by Frank Field (1985) *What Price a Child?* (London, Policy Studies Institute).

49. See *Foster Care: Recommendations on Allowances, Recent Statistics, Financial Information* (1983) (London, National Foster-Care Association).

50. Cassetty (1983), p. 6.

51. Jenny Levin (Oct. 1983), 'After divorce . . .', *Childright*, p. 15.

52. McClements (1978), p. 103.

53. J. Buckle (1984), *Mental Handicap Costs More* (London, Disability Income Group); S. Baldwin (1977), *Disabled Children: Counting the Costs* (London, Disability Alliance).

54. Isabell Sawhill, 'Developing Normative Standards for Child Support Payments', in Cassetty (1983), ch. 7.

55. R. van Slooten and A. G. Coverdale (1978), 'The Characteristics of Low Income Households', *Social Trends*, No. 8 (London, HMSO), pp. 27–9.

56. These figures are derived from Table 7.1: the figure for the children is based on the assumption that the value of unity is the equivalent income scale of a married couple (the wife not working). However, for our purposes we have assumed that the

marginal costs of a child are the same whether the household consists of one or two adults.

57. This formula corresponds with Sawhill's (1983) third formula, in Cassetty (1983), p. 85, Table 7.2.
58. *Social Security in New Zealand* (1972), ch. 12; Peter Townsend (1979), *Poverty in the United Kingdom* (Harmondsworth, Penguin Books), ch. 1.
59. This seems to be the policy adopted in New Zealand: Family Proceedings Act 1980, s. 65 (3).
60. See Finer Report (1974), vol. 1, paras. 4.188–190.
61. *Shallow* v. *Shallow* [1979] Fam. 1; *Tovey* v. *Tovey* (1978) 8 Family Law 80; *Girvan* v. *Girvan* (1983) 13 Family Law 213; *Freeman* v. *Swatridge* (1984) 14 Family Law 214.
62. [1979] Fam. 1.
63. As in *Peacock* v. *Peacock* [1984] 1 All ER 1069.

8. The Maintenance of a Former Spouse

By placing our general assessment of post-divorce maintenance between spouses after our discussion of child support, we deliberately depart from the traditional manner in which financial and property adjustment on divorce has been approached. This is because, as we explained at the outset of the previous chapter, we take the view that the obligation of child support constitutes an independent, and, indeed, prior claim upon available resources on marriage breakdown. In satisfying, as far as may be, this obligation, any additional obligation towards a former spouse will in the normal case be met. However, there are a number of issues of considerable importance that remain to be considered within the context of the claims between the individual adults. The first set of issues concerns the approach that should be taken on the dissolution of a childless marriage. We need also to pay special attention to the more difficult circumstances which arise after the period of child support has come to an end and also where divorce takes place after all the children have reached independence. The latter situation is of particular complexity, because the household composition and its related economics undergo significant changes, often at a time considerably removed from that when the divorce settlement was made.

It will also be in these contexts, rather than in that of child support, that questions of property distribution fall to be considered. There are two reasons for this. The first is that the English courts have not normally considered that divorce is an appropriate occasion to transfer capital from parents to children, although they have power to do this. In *Lord Lilford* v. *Glyn*[1] (a case of an extremely wealthy father), Orr LJ observed that the courts should not attempt to anticipate how a father may wish to pass on his wealth to the next generation. In the more modest case of *Chamberlain* v. *Chamberlain*,[2] the view was expressed that assets are accumulated by the efforts of the adults and, so long as they meet their responsibilities towards their children, the adults are entitled to enjoy them. The result is that the courts will restrict their powers of intervention to ensuring, so far as they can, the 'shelter, food and education'[3] of the children and not concern themselves with their potential claims as *heirs*. The same approach is to be found regarding claims on death. A child may apply for an award to be made to him from the estate of a deceased parent if that parent has failed to make reasonable financial provision for the child, but this means such provision as it would be reasonable for him to receive *for his maintenance.*[4] The law of intestacy too prefers the claim of a surviving spouse to that of the children.[5]

The second reason is that, by its nature, the claim to child support normally attaches against income. A claim to a standard of living requires regular income over time. Only very rarely can this be achieved by a settlement of capital. The major exception to this is, of course, residential property. We have already observed how a settlement between the adults about occupation of the home is frequently based on the objective of providing a home for the children. Such arrangements should therefore primarily be seen as adjuncts to the issue of child support. But the question of what should eventually happen to the home when the children are no longer dependent restores the issue to one between the spouses alone.

I. Childless Divorces

We have observed how childless divorcees seemed able generally to reach a satisfactory settlement of property issues. Often, a jointly owned home was sold and the proceeds shared, or the husband bought out the wife's share. However, there were a number of cases where the husband had been the sole owner, and the wife received no compensating sum from him when the marriage ended, although it is likely that, in strict law, she may have earned a share under the general law of trusts.[6] We suspect that the reason why settlement is relatively common in such cases is that normally each party continues in paid employment during the marriage and retains a degree of economic independence from the other. Savings or investments might be either in joint names or held separately. In either case, few problems arise on divorce. Of course, the longer such a marriage lasts, the more entangled the economic lives of the spouses are likely to become, and the higher the risk of dispute over accumulated assets, on dissolution. Disputes in such cases do come before the courts, which determine them according to the largely discretionary jurisdiction of the Matrimonial Causes Act 1973 as amended by the Matrimonial and Family Proceedings Act 1984.[7] But the difficulty of applying a discretionary jurisdiction in such situations has already been described.[8] It is for reasons such as these that the enactment of a norm of equal division of matrimonial property has seemed to many to be attractive.[9]

We are less convinced of the advantages of adopting such a course. The concept of property division on divorce rests upon an ideological conception of marriage as a partnership. We have noted above that this concept should be approached with caution. Oldham has recently argued that the analogy between marriage and partnership becomes attenuated when there are no children of the marriage, unless the marriage is long-lasting. He accordingly proposes that marital property rights should begin to accrue only after a child is born into the marriage or when the marriage has lasted twenty five years.[10] As will become clear, we think that there are some merits in this kind of approach. At least, we do not detect sufficient need, either in terms of evidence of feelings of injustice over present practice or of difficulties in reaching agreements, for introducing a norm of equal division of matrimonial property in the case of childless marriages to justify confronting the formidable difficulties in formulating the appropriate rules. Indeed, as we argue in the context of pension entitlements,[11] the inclusion of vested pension rights as such property subject to equal division might lead to unwarranted windfalls to the former partners of such marriages.

The major types of case where conflicts may arise are where one spouse has financially contributed to a house which is in the name of the other or has assisted (by paid or unpaid work) in the development of the business endeavours of the other. In either case, legal principles already exist for providing compensation for the contributor according to the value of the contribution, and it seems better to permit settlements on this basis than to hang the threat of equal division of business assets over one of the parties.[12] In any case, we believe the courts should be entitled to fall back on the residual principle persuasively propounded by the Scottish Law Commission that 'where one party has made contributions which have been to the economic benefit of the other party or has sustained economic disadvantages in the interests of the other party or of the family, he should receive due recognition of those contributions or disadvantages'.[13] The difficulties raised by attempting to put a value on the contribution of child caregiving would not, *ex hypothesi*, arise. Such a principle would be adequate to cover possible claims arising at the termination of a long-lasting childless marriage. Since it is likely that in such a case each spouse will have retained a good deal of economic independence, the threat of serious inequity will be somewhat remote and our evidence does not suggest that much litigation is likely from these sources.

Would such a principle be sufficient to form the basis of a claim for continuing support as well as for the distribution of property or payment of a lump sum? We believe that it would. Marriage in itself no longer sets up an obligation on one spouse to maintain the other at a level equivalent to his own, after the union has been dissolved. Our discussion of the 'needs' principle in Chapter 3 drew attention to the difficulties of confining such an obligation to the provision of a former spouse's 'needs'. Since social security law does not regard a former spouse as liable to make recompense for the provision the state makes to meet the other's needs, there is no reason why private maintenance law should, in principle, do so either. We would reject the assumption that seems to have been made in some cases[14] that, by marrying, a man implicitly undertakes to relieve the state of its obligation to provide subsistence to his wife after a divorce, should she become entitled to it. On the other hand, it should be recognized that situations may occur even in childless marriages where one of the spouses has undergone financial detriment which has directly or indirectly conferred economic advantage on the other. These may or may not relate, in the words of the New Zealand legislation, to the 'division of functions' within the marriage.[15] It would therefore seem to be better to leave the basis for any such claim flexible. Nor does it seem possible to provide any coherent set of principles indicating the level of provision which should be made, or its duration. The proper basis for the application of the restitutory principle must relate to the degree of detriment suffered and advantage gained in each particular case.

II. Children divorces

We first consider how questions of property distribution should be approached in divorces involving children. The previous chapter set out the basis on which, in our view, financial provision should be made when one of the adults has care of a dependent child. A principle of equalization should be applied, subject to upper and lower limits. Transfers of large sums of capital will seldom, if ever, be apppropriate for these ends. But the transfer, or other settlement, of a dwelling house could go far towards satisfying the housing costs component in the budget of a family with children. This could safely be left to the criteria governing child support. But, although unusual, there may be cases where assets have been accumulated during the marriage which are excessive to these requirements. Once the claims grounded on child support are satisfied, should there be further distribution of assets between the adults, and, if so on what basis? We will argue shortly for a principle of equality applicable on the joint inception of parenthood. But this principle of partnership, as will be seen, is distinct from a principle of partnership which entails the sharing (under a norm of equality or otherwise) of all assets acquired during the duration of the parenthood. We are far from denying that policy should impose such a principle in such circumstances, although we remain unconvinced about the extent of commitment to it by the better off. To give such rights to each adult goes beyond what we have conceived to be the social obligation to the children and their caregiver. In the absence of any express or implied arrangement between them, we are not sure that the fact of joint parenthood in itself establishes a claim to an equal sharing in all assets, however substantial, should the marriage terminate. But, as in the case of childless marriages, it is important that some accessible mechanism for compensating a former spouse for financial benefits conferred on the other, should be available. The principle of compensation for advantages conferred and disadvantages undergone (other than by way of child caregiving) might be adequate to dispose of any claims that would arise. These cases would be relatively few.

We need now to address the situation which arises when the children are no longer dependent. Our data show that, unless a divorced mother who has been caring for the children remarries, she is very likely to be living well below the average standard of living. She is unlikely to have accumulated much, if anything at all, in the way of savings. She will almost certainly be in an inferior position regarding rights under pension schemes. Her earning capacity can do little to alleviate her position.

Policy must squarely confront the problems raised by the conditions in which these women live. For if the long-term consequences on children of breakdowns in our social system of family-based child-rearing are imperfectly understood, in the case of the women they are clear. Policy might allow the loss to lie where it falls, taking the view that they chose to bear, and rear, children in a society where other opportunities are now available to women, and in so choosing, took the risk that the security offered by a two-earner (or at least, male earner) family might collapse, leaving them in circumstances from which it is virtually impossible to recover. We would reject this solution in the strongest terms. We do not believe that the choice whether or not to bear children can be located within an artificial model of economic rationality. Like the instinct for sexual fulfilment, it is governed by strong biological imperatives. But quite apart from that, no community can survive without the reproduction of its members. The social mechanism by which this is achieved is vital to that community's interests and demands special consideration for those who exercise this function. Finally, the fact that the women bear the risk of the adverse consequences of breakdowns in the system in disproportion to men reflects society's social organization of labour.[16] If men were equally involved in child-rearing, the risks would be more evenly spread. Since the deprivations are, at root, socially caused, society (not the individual women) must bear the responsibility.

Accepting that a special obligation is owed to these women, we must consider how it can be met. It seems to us, as it does in the parallel case of child support, that the burden of this insurance should prima facie lie on the state. This has been accepted in New Zealand, where a special benefit, equivalent to widows' benefit, is payable to an applicant who, even if not presently caring for a child, has exercised such care (or care over an incapacitated relative) for fifteen years.[17] As in all cases where state benefits are payable, problems of setting its level and consequential difficulties over equity between competing claimant groups, inevitably arise. It is difficult to resist the argument that the former caregiver's standard of living should be no lower than that set by an appropriate norm for women in that particular age group who have exercised equivalent care but whose marriages remain intact. This may leave (her) better off than various other potential claimants on state benefits, but this should not deter recognition of this significant group of people. If such a benefit existed, should the state have a right of recourse against the former spouse? We recall our observation[18] that the basis for the state's right of recourse in the case of child support is different from the rationale for a direct claim between child and parent. The state's interests lie in revenue collection and, possibly, influencing behaviour. The case for the pursuance of either of these interests by recourse against a former spouse in the situation under consideration seems weak, especially if he has in the past made contribution to child support. Under the New Zealand scheme there is no provision for the state to have recourse against a liable relative except where benefits are paid to parents who have care of children who are currently dependent.

It is doubtful, in the light of experience, and current political and economic trends, whether a satisfactory outcome through state funding will be achieved easily. As in the case of child support, we need to look for other resources to satisfy, as far as may be, the former caregiver's claim. We would here propose a model which sees child-rearing during marriage as a joint enterprise, under which the risks of failure should be borne by each of the adults equally. We could say that this is the very essence of the family-based system. Even if the parties themselves do not conceptualize it as such, the *de facto* nature of the enterprise can be said to form a principled basis for a claim by one former spouse against the other which seeks to neutralize the imbalance of risk generated by our social organization. It is in this sense that we can refer to parenthood as a partnership, and it is on this basis that we contend that the resources of a former spouse may be held available for the benefit of the caregiver of their common children when caregiving is completed. But although the principle seems (to us) to be clear, we should warn at the outset that there are considerable practical difficulties in finding a satisfactory solution through private law.

One major difficulty lies in the fact that the extent of the former caregiver's claim to redress these risks depends on the economic circumstances of each party *when caregiving finishes*. Both the legitimacy of the claim, and problems in its satisfaction, have been evident in the concern the courts have felt with respect to a former wife's accommodation prospects when the children have grown up. The device, known as the 'Mesher' order,[19] whereby the matrimonial home is settled on trust for sale, with sale postponed until the youngest child has left school (during which period the wife and children were given the right to occupy the house) has been subjected to repeated criticism on the grounds that to sell the house at that stage could severely prejudice the former wife's position regarding accommodation.[20] One solution is to extend the woman's occupational rights for the period of her life, or some other event (like remarriage, or voluntary vacation of the premises), perhaps requiring her to pay rent to her former husband during this period. Another is to transfer the house outright to the wife at the time of the divorce.[21] The difficulty about these solutions is that the courts have attempted to anticipate, at the time of divorce, what the circumstances may be a number of years hence. The failure to do this adequately was the cause of dissatisfaction over 'Mesher' orders themselves. It is not clear that the alternatives available are always appropriate to the circumstances which later arise. Even if sale of the house is not required when the children leave and the wife is permitted to stay, the low level of her income may make it very difficult for her to meet the routine costs of occupation and may impair its eventual market value. Yet, once a property adjustment order is made, it cannot subsequently be varied.[22] This restriction reflected the Law Commission's view that property adjustments were not primarily intended to correct any imbalance between the parties' means and needs, but to reflect the true position at the time of divorce.[23] This perception rests on an inadequate appreciation of the longer term consequences of divorce and the effects which property settlement can have on them. There is indeed no reason why an attempt should not be made to settle matters finally at the time the divorce is granted, but in our view the economic transition at completion of child caregiving is so profound that the situation should always in principle be subject to review at that stage, even in regard to property matters. Although this might seem to enhance the risks of later litigation and to fly in the face of the policy of promoting once-and-for-all settlements, we would observe that it would apply only at the completion of a period of child caregiving, during which financial provisions are always in principle subject to review. More importantly, however, we proceed to suggest principles upon which post-caregiving support might be calculated which would greatly reduce the scope for conflict and could indeed be incorporated in original divorce settlements.

If a residence, derived from the former marriage, is to be held available to a former wife at this stage, can a claim to other property be sustained? Can we argue, following Oldham,[24] that the partnership implied in entry into joint parenthood entitles a share, perhaps an equal share, in assets existing either at the time of divorce (or even, on a stronger view, at the time of cessation of child caregiving)? We have already dismissed the argument that the partnership of parenthood necessarily entails this conclusion. What the woman stands to lose by extended absence from employment due to child caregiving is not equal participation in the fruits of her husband's income or the family assets built up by the income of both, but the difference between what she will in fact be able to earn on re-entry into employment and what she would have earned had she not left it. This is because, unless the ideology of partnership is imposed on all marriages, including those without children, if the marriage had been childless, she would have been left to rely on her own earning capacity.

The conclusion from this reasoning is that the loss for which the woman should be compensated is the degree to which her eventual standard of living after caregiving falls short of what she might have expected *had the marriage broken down without caregiving*. This is the risk which usually falls unequally on the wife, and the principle of equal risk sharing demands that this loss should be distributed proportionately between them. Others have found this argument attractive.[25] We adverted in Chapter 3 to the considerable difficulties in the way of its practical application. What degree of confidence can be placed in speculating what any individual woman's financial position would have been if she had not modified her employment activities as a result of child-rearing, even though economists are attempting to calculate such losses in general terms.[26] What weight is to be put on the speculations that, if the marriage in question had been childless, and broken down, the woman may have entered another marriage (successfully or unsuccessfully, with or without children)? Should the actual benefits of child-rearing be evaluated and offset against her losses? If so, how?. These difficulties are too profound to permit such lost opportunity costs to form an acceptable basis for attacking the former spouse's resources. We need to look to an alternative mode of assessment which represents a reasonable compromise between the principle we have accepted and the real problems of assessment, acceptability, and enforceability.

This alternative might be found in the concept of the 'norm' applied to standard of living. The equalization of risks of a parenthood jointly undertaken establishes a prima facie claim to the richer parent's resources. If those resources are sufficient, we can argue that the former caregiver should be entitled to draw on them to keep her standard of living as close as possible to the chosen 'norm' for a two-adult family at the equivalent state in its life-cycle. How should this normative standard be established? It might seem logical to choose the standard set by the norm during the period of child support. The difficulty with this solution is that the standard of living of most families does not remain constant. In the ordinary course of events, the emergence of children from dependence coincides with the peak in earnings attained during the ages of forty to forty-nine.[27] A married couple can usually look forward to an increase in their living standards at about that time, although this will usually suffer a marked decline after the ages of fifty and, particularly, sixty. These difficulties are exacerbated by marked divergences between occupational groups.

If the standard were to be sensitive to these fluctuations, it would need to be related to the age of the claimant and possibly the occupational category of the payer. This could be incorporated into a set of standards by which maintenance arrangements were to be assessed. We would favour a single standard, adjusting automatically at the ages of forty, fifty, and sixty. The consequence would be that, in cases where the payer had the resources to satisfy the claim to the full extent of the standard, the recipient would be faced with reductions of maintenance after reaching fifty and sixty, which might or might not reflect the payer's ability to pay in the particular case. Such apparent anomalies would, in our view, be justified in the context of the overall justice of the scheme which seeks to meet, so far as possible from private resources, the minimal claims of the former caregiver, while at the same time respecting a degree of economic independence for the payer. It should be observed that the new basis for calculating the standard on the cessation of child support would not necessarily lead to much, if any, increase in the sums paid by the payer. There are two reasons for this. First, the claimant has only herself to support. If the norm for the two adult household, without children, in their forties is 180, the claimant's entitlement would be to only 61 per cent of that.[28] Second, the expectation that she should earn is no longer qualified by reference to child care responsibilities. However, as we observed in our data on these women, this is the point at which they are most vulnerable.

As in the case of child support, the norm is used only to set a standard. If the payer cannot bring the claimant up to it without himself falling below it, we need to consider what lower limits should be set to the obligation. Here again, the principle of joint parenthood seems to demand an equality between the households, subject to a minimum, in the case of the payer, based on the supplementary benefit 'formula' coupled with a disregard.[29] In comparing the two, full account is of course taken of the household composition of each.[30] But at this point we must recognize a problem which faces the use of private law in this area in a particularly acute way, which is, or should be, absent from considerations of child support. It is inevitable that some payers will wish to argue that they should be released from this obligation on account of the misconduct of their former spouse. If we may express this objection in the terms of our conceptualization of this obligation, the argument is that, although the risks of the consequences of parenthood might be jointly undertaken, one of the parties has unilaterally brought about the events against which the imposition of the support obligation seeks to insure.

The question of conduct was described by the Law Commission in its 1981 paper as 'intractable'. They felt, on the one hand, that the legal system was ill-adapted for apportioning responsibility for marital breakdown. On the other hand, they considered that it should remain open to judges, by means of their acquisition of the 'feel' of a particular case, to determine whether it fell into the category of those exceptional cases where it would be 'inequitable' to ignore conduct in the assessment of post-divorce financial obligation.[31] The question of conduct was much debated during the passage of the Matrimonial and Family Proceedings Act 1984, which (preserving the existing law)[32]requires courts, in making financial provision, to have regard to 'the conduct of the parties, if that conduct is such that it would in the opinion of the court be inequitable to disregard it'.[33] The open-ended discretionary nature of this provision is in line with the policy of the whole Act of leaving the difficult decisions to subjective judgment by judges and registrars. But even the question of conduct can be subjected to principled elaboration.

We have already stated (in Chapter 7) that it would in our view be wrong to reduce child support on account of parental misconduct. Nor is marital misconduct likely to be relevant to the restitutory basis of adjustment which we suggest for childless divorces. Such exclusions would go far to limit the potential scope for disputes over conduct. However, we are less certain about the propriety of excluding such matters in relation to the spousal claim after child caregiving is finished. If permitted in this context, however, it should be limited to the extent to which the conduct could be characterized as a repudiation of the principle of joint parenthood. Hence, if the marriage breaks down after child caregiving has been completed with respect to at least one child, conduct cannot be so characterized, for the wife has undergone the events with respect to which the risks have been shared. The difficult case is where (to put it strongly) the wife leaves the husband without good reason during the course of raising the children. Can she not be said to have taken upon herself the risks of adversity when caregiving is complete? But if the repudiation was his, her entitlement should remain intact. As unsatisfactory as it may seem to raise such issues, we can see no escape from them so long as insurance against the cost of failures of the family system is thrown on individuals. This also accords with the strong expression of common sentiment.[34] But the costs in terms of stress on the individuals and children, and on the legal system itself, may be considerable. All we can do is to devise means of mitigating these ills.

The most complete way in which such problems might be reduced would be to relate the extent of the maintenance entitlement to the number of years spent bringing up children. Full entitlement, we might say, would be earned only after (perhaps) sixteen years of child caregiving had been completed. A shorter period would lead to *pro rata* reduction. If the marriage had broken down before the caregiving period had been completed, but it was eventually completed in full, the non-caregiving parent should still retain the prima facie obligation to pay post-caregiving maintenance to the other, but should be allowed to argue that the failure of the common parenting was due to its repudiation by the caregiver. If (he) establishes this (and we do not suppose it would be easy), he should nevertheless remain obliged to pay a proportion of the maintenance corresponding to the length of time which the marriage lasted, but would be absolved from any higher obligation. The result would be that the longer the marriage lasts, the smaller would be the amount at stake, and accordingly at risk of such dispute. Rather than run the risks of such uncertain litigation, parties would be expected to settle the matter.

Our discussion has proceeded on the assumption that the mother would normally remain the caregiver and would wish to make the claim for post-caregiving support. But this might not always be the case. Suppose, after caregiving had ended and the parties were living apart, the husband fell on evil days and his former wife enjoyed a better living standard than he did. It may be difficult to make the assumption of a direct relationship between his present position and his past role in the joint parenthood, but it may nevertheless exist. His commitments to his family life might have also been purchased at some cost to his career opportunities. Such matters cannot easily be investigated, but in principle we believe that the fact of joint parenting should raise a *reciprocal* obligation, so far as is practicable, for the better-off parent to support the other, in the manner described, in the post-caregiving period.

III. Pensions and Insurance

The loss by a divorced woman of the prospects of participation in the fruits of her husband's superannuation or life insurance schemes has long been recognized as a serious deprivation. In 1969, the Law Commission could suggest no satisfactory answer to the problem[35] and nor could the Finer Committee contribute to its solution.[36] A property-based approach to post-divorce settlement inclines towards the inclusion of such entitlements among the matrimonial property subject to division. This requires assessment of the value of these rights which had been built up during the marriage and the allocation of their value at the time of divorce on a once-and-for-all basis between parties.[37] Yet it should be clear that this solution, remote as it is from the real problems of post-divorce economic life, cannot provide a satisfactory result. It may, as the Occupational Pensions Board observed in 1976,[38] overcompensate 'young, childless wives', while at the same time provide insufficiently for the child caregiver in her old age. Furthermore, it subjects the problem to a conceptual straight-jacket. Can a policy which has no cash surrender value properly be considered as matrimonial property? American courts have thought not.[39] Where the rights accrue only on death or retirement, their quantification in terms of matrimonial property accrued at the time of divorce could prove impossible in practice, and attempts to implement them could be very unwieldy.[40]

We would prefer to see the problem of pensions in the context of post child-caregiving support. As the Occupational Pensions Board pointed out,[41] income from a subject's personal pension is simply part of his resources from which maintenance may be ordered. The only adjustment that needs to be made, therefore, concerns the normative standard applicable when the wife reaches retirement age. This needs to be considered with some care. The incomes of retired households differ sharply according to whether they derive primarily from the state pension scheme or from other sources (earnings or a private pension scheme).[42] Nevertheless, in principle we think that the standard should lie between the two levels. This opportunity to share, to some extent, in their former husband's post-retirement earnings or superannuation benefits, may place some divorced wives at a standard of living above many other divorced and non-divorced people living at the level of state retirement pensions or supplementary benefit. Yet this is not unreasonable. They would not, by definition, be living as well as many other former child caregivers whose marriages have lasted into their retirement. The fact that a former husband is a beneficiary of such benefits indicates that the former wife would have participated in a higher living standard had the marriage not broken down. The limitations of the former wife's entitlement to the standard deprives her of possible participation in the full benefits of a high post-retirement income, but this is consistent with our approach of removing any necessary link between the divorced wife's entitlements and her former husband's post-divorce level of resources. It would seem unobjectionable in this context if the divorce had occurred some, perhaps many, years before the retirement. Doubts might be expressed about its equity if a rich man divorced his wife shortly before retiring on the ground that she would be threatened with a severe *drop* in living standards. The case could be met by retaining judicial discretion to override the upper limit in exceptional cases, although our inclination would be to maintain our principle even in this situation. Such a wife is very likely to have resources of her own which would assure her a standard above the norm in any event.

Life policies raise slightly different problems. In 1976 the Government Actuary calculated the extent of benefits lost by widows according to the age and income of their husband at divorce. At age forty, she lost £2,000 if he was earning £3,000 per annum, and £6,000 if he was earning £10,000.[43] But since such benefits depend on her survival of her husband, they cannot form part of the settlement made at divorce. We prefer to avoid approaching the issue on the basis of accrued property rights. Instead, it should be open to parties arranging a divorce to consider whether the husband should take out, or continue, a life policy on such terms as would insure to his former wife, on his death, an income which will keep her at the relevant norm or its capitalized equivalent. Courts do not presently possess powers to require a party to a divorce to execute such a policy,[44] and the Occupational Pensions Board recommended that they should have them.[45] The normative standard would be easily ascertainable, and the amount of the premiums simply calculated. In so far as a husband's premium payments might reduce the income out of which current maintenance or child support must be found, it would be a question of judgement in many cases whether such an arrangement would be in the claimant's interests. We found that such issues never entered into the contemplation of our older divorcees at the time they divorced and it is unlikely that resources existed in most cases to achieve any benefit. However, where the former husband has such resources, there seems no reason why such provisions should not form part of the standard divorce settlement. In such a case we do not think that premium payments should be treated as equivalent to maintenance or child support payments and should not, therefore, reduce the level of these payments properly payable under the appropriate standard.

We need now to summarize the position to which our arguments have taken us. The private-law obligation of post-divorce maintenance is seen essentially as a mechanism for making good, out of private resources, an obligation owed by the community to those who have cared for children. This both establishes, and limits, the obligation. Since the concern is with living standards, we have eschewed questions of distribution by right of property entitlement. Of course capital (in particular, residential accommodation) may be distributed by way of full or part satisfaction of the long-term obligation. This will, as our data show, exhaust the readily available assets in almost all cases. Where either party holds assets beyond what is necessary to achieve these ends, any basis for their acquisition by the other spouse must rest on a different principle. The ideology of partnership, whether arising by the fact of marriage, or later, for example, on the inception of parenthood, could provide such a basis. While we have no strong grounds for opposing this ideology, we are less enthusiastic about it than many commentators. Our preference lies in the establishment of a firm principle of compensation for advantages conferred and detriments suffered which could have application in a relatively limited, but important, number of situations. While the jurisdiction in this context would retain a degree of discretionary flexibility which presently permeates the whole approach to post-divorce maintenance, it is unlikely seriously to undermine the scope for settled agreements. The major areas where such maintenance is of importance to the parties would be covered by a series of readily ascertainable standards, calculated to make good, so far as private law and individual resources can, the shortfall in the community's obligations both to its children and their caregivers, without intruding excessively into the individualist values represented by the right to divorce and establish serial families.

Notes

1. [1979] 1 WLR 78.
2. [1973] 1 WLR 1557.
3. See *Harnett* v. *Harnett* [1973] Fam. 156, at p. 161, per Bagnall J. See also *Griffiths* v. *Griffiths* [1984] 3 WLR 165, where it was emphasized that a property order in favour of children might be made if this was necessary to discharge the parental responsibility to provide proper care.
4. Inheritance (Provision for Family and Dependents) Act 1975, s. 1 (1), (2); the courts will be slow to entertain a claim by an able-bodied child of full age: *re Coventry (dec'd)* [1979] 3 All ER 815.
5. See Mary Ann Glendon (1981), *The New Family: and the New Property* (Toronto, Butterworth), p. 22.
6. *Gissing* v. *Gissing* [1970] AC 777.
7. *Potter* v. *Potter* [1982] 3 All ER 321 is a recent example.
8. See above, p. 45.
9. Scottish Law Commission (1981), *Family Law: Report on Aliment and Financial Provision*, Scot. Law Com. No. 67, paras. 366–7; Ruth Deech (1982), 'Financial Relief: The Retreat from Precedent and Principle', 98 *Law Quarterly Rev.* 621–55; Mary Ann Glendon (1981), 'Property Rights upon Dissolution of Marriages and Informal Unions', in Nancy E. Eastham and Boris Krivy (eds.), *The Cambridge Lectures 1981 (London, Butterworths)*. In this lecture, Glendon advocates the separate treatment, as proposed in this book, of marriages which have produced children from those which have not.

10. J. Thomas Oldham (1983–4), 'Is the Concept of Marital Property Outdated?', *22 Journal of Family Law*, 263.

11. See below, pp. 149–52.

12. See Scot. Law Com. No. 67, paras. 3.69–72.

13. Scot. Law Com. No. 67, para. 3.99.

14. See Chapter 3, n. 4.

15. Family Proceedings Act 1980, s. 60 (1) (a).

16. For a general critique, see Frances E. Olsen (1983), 'The Family and the Market: A Study of Ideology and Legal Reform', 96 *Harvard Law Rev.*, 1497–578, esp. p. 1547.

17. Social Security Amendment Act 1973, s. 6, inserting s. 27C into the Social Security Act 1964.

18. See above, pp. 111–2.

19. After its use in *Mesher* v. *Mesher*, a 1973 case reported in [1980] 1 All ER 126.

20. *Harvey* v. *Harvey* [1982] 2 Fam. 83; *Carson* v. *Carson* [1983] 1 WLR 285; *Tinsdale* v. *Tinsdale* (1983) 13 Family Law 148.

21. *Hanlon* v. *Hanlon* [1978] 1 WLR 592; this however failed to protect the wife because the legal aid fund acquired a first charge on the proceeds of sale of the house: *Hanlon* v. *Law Society* [1981] AC 124; see Deech (1982) at p. 634.

22. Matrimonial Causes Act 1973, s. 24 (1) (b); *Carson* v. *Carson* [1983] 1 WLR 285; *Norman* v. *Norman* [1983] 1 All ER 486.

23. Law Commission (1969), *Family Law: Report on Financial Provision in Matrimonial Proceedings*, Law Com. No. 25, para. 87.

24. See above, note 10.

25. See J. Cassetty (1983), *The Parental Child Support Obligation* (Lexington, Lexington Books), pp. 91–3; Hilaire Barnett (1983), 'Financial Provision — A Compensatory Model?', 13 *Family Law*, 124.

26. See for example H. Joshi (1985), *The Price of Parenthood*, Paper presented at the Centre for Economic Policy Research, claiming that mothers lose £50,000 in lifetime earnings raising two children.

27. *New Earnings Survey*, 1980 (Department of Employment, London, HMSO).

28. See above, Table 7.1.

29. See above, p. 128.

30. See the formulae on p. 119.

31. Law Commission (1981), *Family Law: The Financial Consequences of Divorce*, Law Com. No. 112, paras. 36–9.

32. See *Robinson* v. *Robinson* [1983] 1 All ER 391.

33. Matrimonial Causes Act 1973, s. 25 (2) (g) as amended by the Matrimonial and Family Proceedings Act 1984, s. 3.

34. See R. Jowell and C. Airey (1984), *British Social Attitudes* (London, Gower), p. 140.

35. Law Com. No. 25, p. 53.

36. *Report of the Committee on One-Parent Families* (Finer Report) (1974), Cmnd. 5629, vol. 1, para. 5.304.

37. Scot. Law Com. No. 67, para. 3.73.

38. *Report on the Occupational Pensions Board* (1976), Cmnd. 6599 (London, HMSO), ch. 13, para. 13.48.

39. See M. R. Brown (1983–4), 'Whose Life (Insurance) is it Anyway? Life Insurance and Divorce in America', 22 *Jo. Fam. Law*, 95–128.

40. The Scottish Law Commission envisage orders for capital sum payments either at divorce or in the future in such cases: Scot Law Com. No. 67, para. 3.74. But it is

unclear how the calculation of such sums is to be related to the 'accrued value' during the subsistence of the marriage.

41. Op. cit. para. 13.68.
42. *Family Expenditure Survey, 1982* (London HMSO).
43. (1976), Cmnd. 6599, ch. 13, Table 18.
44. *Milne* v. *Milne, The Times,* 6 Feb. 1981.
45. (1976), Cmnd. 6599, ch. 13, para. 13.55.

Table of Cases

Table of Statutes

Bibliography

Agell, A. ((1979), 'Social Security and Family Law in Sweden', in A. Samuels (ed.) *Social Security and Family Law* (UK Comparative Law Series, No.4)

Alberta Institute for Law Research and Reform (1974), *Matrimonial Property, Working Paper*

Anderson, M. (1971), *Family Structure in Nineteenth Century Lancashire* (Cambridge, Cambridge University Press)

Anderson, M. (1979), 'The relevance of family history' in M. Anderson (ed.), *The Sociology of the Family* (Harmondsworth, Penguin Books)

Anderson, Stuart (1984), 'Legislative Divorce – Law for the Aristocracy?' in G.R. Rubin and David Sugarman (eds.) *Law, Economy and Society: Essays in the History of English Law* (Abingdon, Professional Books)

Atkin, W.R. (1981), 'Liable Relatives: The New State Role in Ordering Maintenance', 5 *Otago Law Rev.*, 48

Atkin, W.R. (1981) 'Spousal Maintenance: A New Philosophy?', 9 *NZ Universities Law Rev.*, 336

Atkins, E., N.M. Cherry, J.W.B. Douglas, E. Kienard, and M.E.J. Wadsworth (1981), 'Progress and Results of the National Survey of Health and Development', in S.A. Mednick and A.E. Baird (eds.), *An Empirical Basis for Primary Prevention* (Oxford, Oxford University Press)

Baldwin, S. (1977), *Disabled Children: Counting the Costs* (London, Disability Alliance)

Barnett, Hilaire (1983), 'Financial Provision – A Compensatory Model?', 13 *Family Law*, 124

Barrington-Baker, W., John Eekelaar, Colin Gibson, and Susan Raikes (1977), *The Matrimonial Jurisdiction of Registrars* (Oxford, SSRC Centre for Socio-Legal Studies.

Beckerman, Wilfred and Stephen Clark (1982), *Poverty and Social Security in Britain since 1961* (Oxford, Oxford University Press)

Blackstone, William (1765), *Commentaries on the Laws of England*

Broun, Malcolm D. (1981), 'Financial Implications of Family Law', 55 *Australian Law Journal*, 424

Brown, L. Neville (1955), 'National Assistance and the Liability to

Maintain One's Family' 18 *Modern Law Rev.*, 110–19

Brown, M.R. (1983–4), 'Whose Life (Insurance) is it Anyway? Life Insurance and Divorce in America', 22 *Jo.Fam. Law*, 95–128

Bruch, Carol (1983), 'Child Support Payments: A Critique', in Judith Cassetty (ed.) *The Parental Child-Support Obligation* (Lexington, Lexington Books)

Buckle, J. (1984), *Mental Handicap Costs More* (London, Disability Income Group)

Cassetty, Judith (1983), 'Emerging Issues in Child-Support Policy and Practice', in Judith Cassetty (ed.), *The Parental Child-Support Obligation* (Lexington, Lexington Books)

Chambers, David (1979), *Making Fathers Pay: The Enforcement of Child Support* (Chicago, University of Chicago Press)

Cherlin, A. (1981), *Marriage, Divorce, Remarriage* (Cambridge, Harvard University Press)

Chester, Robert (1971), 'The Duration of Marriage to Divorce', 22 *British Journal of Sociology*, 172

Chisholm, Richard and Owen Jessup (1981), 'Fault and Financial Adjustment under the Family Law Act', 4 *University of NSW Law Journal*, No.2, 43

Crozier, Blanche (1935), 'Marital Support', 15 *Boston ULR*, 28.

Daniel, W. (1981), *The Unemployed Flow* (London, Policy Studies Institute)

Davis, Gwyn, Alison Macleod, and Mervyn Murch (1983), 'Divorce: Who Supports the Family?', 13 *Family Law*, 217

Deech, Ruth (1982), 'Financial Relief: The Retreat from Precedent and Principle', 98 *Law Quarterly Rev.* 621–55

Dingwall, R.W.J., J.M. Eekelaar and Topsy Murray (1984), 'Childhood as a Social Problem: A Survey of the History of Legal Regulation', 2 *Journal of Law and Society*, 207–82

Doig, B. (1982), *The Nature and Scale of Aliment and Financial Provision on Divorce in Scotland* (Edinburgh Central Research Unit, Scottish Office)

Donajgrodzki, A.P. (1977), 'Social Police and the Bureaucratic Elite: A Vision of Order in an Age of Reform', in A.P. Donajgrodzki (ed.), *Social Control in Nineteenth Century Britain* (London, Croom Helm)

Donzelot, J. (1980), *The Policing of Families* (London, Hutchinson)

Dopfel, Peter and Bernard Buchhofer (1983), *Unterhaltsrecht in Europa* (Tubingen, J.C.B. Mohr)

Douglas, J. (1970), 'Broken Families and Child Behaviour', 4 *Journal of the Royal College of Physicians*, 203–10

Edgell, Stephen (1980), *Middle Class Couples* (London, George Allen and Unwin)

Editorial Note (1983), 13 *Family Law* 84

Eekelaar, J.M. (1979), 'Some Principles of Financial and Property Adjustment on Divorce', 95 *Law Quarterly Rev.* 253–69

Eekelaar, John (1984), *Family Law and Social Policy* (2nd edn.) (London, Weidenfeld and Nicolson)

Eekelaar, John and Eric Clive, with Karen Clarke and Susan Raikes (1977), *Custody after Divorce* (Oxford, SSRC Centre for Socio-Legal Studies)

Eekelaar, J.M., R.M.J. Dingwall and T. Murray (1982), 'Victims or Threats: Children in Care Proceedings', *Journal of Social Welfare Law*, 68–82

Elias, Peter and Brian Main (n.d.), *Women's Working Lives: Evidence from the National Training Survey* (University of Warwick Institute for Employment Research)

Ferri, Elsa (1976), *Growing-up in a One-Parent Family* (London, National Council for Educational Research in England and Wales)

Field, Frank (1985), *What Price a Child?* (London, Policy Studies Institute)

Finer, Morris and O.R. McGregor (1974), 'The History of the Obligation to Maintain', in *Report of the Committee on One-Parent Families*, Cmnd. 5629, vol.2, Appendix 5 (London, HMSO)

Finlay, H.A. (1979), *Family Law in Australia* (2nd. edn.) (Sydney, Butterworths)

Foster Care: Recommendations on Allowances, Recent Statistics, Financial Information (London, National Foster Care Association)

Gibson, Colin (1974), 'The Association between Divorce and Social Class in England and Wales', 25 *British Journal of Sociology*, 79

Gibson, Colin (1982), 'Maintenance in the Magistrates' Courts in the 1980s', 12 *Family Law*, 138

Glendon, Mary Ann (1976), 'Marriage and the State: The Withering Away of Marriage', 62 *Virginia LR*, 663–706

Glendon, Mary Ann (1981), *The New Family and the New Property* (Toronto, Butterworths)

Glendon, Mary Ann (1981), 'Property Rights upon Dissolution of Marriages and Informal Unions' in Nancy E. Eastham and Boris Krivy (eds.), *The Cambridge Lectures 1981* (London, Butterworths)

Goode, W. (1956), *After Divorce* (New York, The Free Press)

Gray, Kevin (1977) *The Reallocation of Property on Divorce* (Abingdon, Professional Books)

Harris, C.C. (1983), *The Family and Industrial Society* (London, George Allen and Unwin)

Haskey, John (1983), 'Children of Divorcing Couples', *Population Trends* No. 31 (London, HMSO)

Hayes, Mary (1983), 'Maintenance Defaulters – Are Poor Men Wrongfully sent to Prison?', 13 *Family Law*, 243–8

Hoffman, Saul (1977), 'Marital Instability and the Economic Status of Women', 14 *Demography*, 67

Hofstadter, Samuel F. and Shirley R. Levittan (1967), 'Alimony – A Reformulation', 7 *Journal of Family Law*, 51

Joshi, H. (1985), *The Price of Parenting* (London, Centre for Economic Policy Research)

Jowell, R. and C. Airey (1984), *British Social Attitudes* (London, Gower)

Kellmer Pringle, M. (ed.) (1980), *The Needs of Children* (London, Hutchinson)

Knetsch, Jack L. (1984), 'Some Economic Implications of Matrimonial Property Rules', 34 *University of Toronto Law Journal*, 263–82

Land, Hilary (1975), 'The Introduction of Family Allowances: An Act of Historical Justice?' in P. Hall et al., *Change, Choice and Conflict in Social Policy* (London, Heinemann)

Land, Hilary (1983), 'Poverty and Gender', in M. Brown (ed.), *The Structure of Disadvantage* (London, Heinemann)

Law Commission (1969), *Family Law: Report on Financial Provision in Matrimonial Proceedings*, Law Com. No. 25 (London, HMSO)

Law Commission (1980), *Family Law: The Financial Consequences of Divorce: The Basic Policy*, Law Com. No. 103 (London, HMSO)

Law Commission (1981), *Family Law: the Financial Consequences of Divorce*, Law Com. No. 112 (London, HMSO)

Law Reform Commission of Canada (1975), *Maintenance on Divorce*, Working Paper No. 12 (Ottawa, Information Canada)

Law Reform Commission of Canada (1976), *Family Law* (Ottawa, Information Canada)

Layard, Richard (1978), 'The Causes of Poverty', *Royal Commission on the Distribution of Income and Wealth*, Background Paper No. 6 (London, HMSO)

Lee, B.H. (1974), *Divorce Reform in England* (London, Peter Owen)

Leete, Richard (1979), *Changing Patterns of Family Formation and Dissolution in England and Wales 1964–76* (Office of Population, Censuses and Surveys, London, HMSO)

Leete, R. and S. Anthony (1979), 'Divorce and Remarriage: A Record Linkage Study', 16 *Population Trends* (London, HMSO)

Levin, Jennifer (1978), 'Direct Maintenance Payments to Children', 8 *Family Law*, 195–8

Levin, Jennifer (1983), 'After divorce . . .', *Childright*, 15

Maclean, Mavis and Hazel Genn (1979), *Methodological Issues in Social Surveys* (London, Macmillan)

Maclean, Mavis and John Eekelaar (1983), *Children and Divorce: Economic Factors* (Oxford, SSRC Centre for Socio-Legal Studies)

Maidment, Susan (1984), *Child Custody and Divorce* (Beckenham, Croom Helm)

Malmstrom, A. (1955), 'Sweden' in W. Friedmann (ed.), *Matrimonial Property Law* (London, Stevens)

Manners, A.J. and I. Rauta (1981), *Family Property in Scotland* (London, HMSO)

Mansfield, Penny (1982), *The Guardian*, 9 February

Marsden, D. (1973), *Mothers Alone* (Harmondsworth, Penguin Books)

Martin, Jean (1984), *Women and Employment* (Office of Population, Censuses and Surveys, London, HMSO)

McClements, Leslie (1978), *The Economics of Social Security* (London, Heinemann)

McGregor, O.R. (1957), *Divorce in England: A Centenary Study* (London, Heinemann)

McGregor, O.R., L. Blom-Cooper, and C. Gibson (1970), *Separated Spouses* (London, Duckworth)

McLanahan, Sara (1985), 'Family Structure and the Reproduction of Poverty', 90 *American Journal of Sociology*, 873

Merrett, S. and F. Gray (1982), *Owner Occupation in Britain* (London, Routledge and Kegan Paul)

Murie, A. (1983), *Housing, Inequality and Deprivation* (London, Heinemann)

Oldham, J. Thomas (1983–4), 'Is the Concept of Marital Property Outdated?', 22 *Journal of Family Law*, 263

Olsen, Frances E. (1983), 'The Family and the Market: A Study of Ideology and Legal Reform', 96 *Harvard Law Rev.* 1497–578

Ontario Law Reform Commission (1975), *Report on Family Law, Part VI: Support Obligations*

Pahl, Jan (1980), 'Patterns of Money Management within Marriage', 9 *Journal of Social Policy*, 313–17

Parliamentary Debates (1984), *Special Standing Committee, Matrimonial and Family Proceedings Bill* (London, HMSO)

Phillips (1929), *The Practice of the Divorce Division*

Piachaud, David (1979), *The Cost of a Child: A Modern Minimum*

(London, Child Poverty Action Group)

Pinchbeck, I. and M. Hewitt (1969), *Children in English Society* (London, Routledge and Kegan Paul)

Popay, Jennie, Lesley Rimmer, and Chris Rossiter (1983), *One Parent Families: Parents, Children and Public Policy* (London, Study Commission on the Family)

Pottick, E.J. (1978), 'Tort Damages for the Injured Homemaker: Opportunity Cost or Replacement Cost?', 50 *University of Colorado Law Rev.* 59

Poynter's Law of Marriage and Divorce (1824)

Rayden on Divorce, (6th edn.) (1953) (London, Butterworths)

Rea, Samuel A. (1984), 'Taxes, Transfers and the Family', 34 *University of Toronto Law Journal*, 314–40

Report of the Commission of Inquiry into Poverty in Australia (1975) (Canberra, Australian Government Publishing Service)

Report of the Commissioners on the Practice and Jurisdiction of the Ecclesiastical Courts in England and Wales, Parliamentary Papers, 1831–2, vol. 24

Report of the Committee on One-Parent Families, (1974) Cmnd. 5629 (London, HMSO)

Report of the Committee on Statutory Maintenance Limits (1968) Cmnd. 3587 (London, HMSO)

Report of the Joint Select Committee on the Family Law Act (1980) (Canberra, Australian Government Publishing Service)

Report of the Occupational Pensions Board (1976) Cmnd. 6599 (London, HMSO)

Report from His Majesty's Commissioners for Inquiring into the Administration and Practical Operation of the Poor Law, Parliamentary Papers 1834, vol.44

Rosen, Harvey (1974), 'The Monetary Value of a Housewife: A Replacement Cost Approach', *American Journal of Economics and Society*, 65

Rowntree, G. (1955), 'Early Childhood in Broken Families', 8 *Population Studies*, 247

Royal Commission of Inquiry: Social Security in New Zealand (1972) (Wellington, Government Printer)

Royal Commission on Family and Children's Law, Seventh Report, Family Maintenance (1975) (Victoria, Government of British Columbia)

Royal Commission on Marriage and Divorce (1956) Cmnd. 9678 (London, HMSO)

Sawhill, Isabel (1983), 'Developing Normative Standards for Child-Support Payments' in Judith Cassetty (ed.), *The Parental Child-*

Support Obligation (Lexington, Lexington Books)

Schmidt, Folke (1971), 'The Prospective Law of Marriage', *Scandinavian Studies in Law*, 193–218

Schmidt, Svenne (1984), 'The Scandinavian Law of Procedure and Matrimonial Causes', in John M. Eekelaar and Sanford N. Katz (eds.), *The Resolution of Family Conflict: Comparative Legal Perspectives* (Toronto, Butterworths)

Scottish Law Commission (1976), *Family Law: Aliment and Financial Provision*, Memorandum No.22 (London, HMSO)

Scottish Law Commission (1981), *Family Law: Report on Aliment and Financial Provision*, Scot. Law Com. No. 67 (London, HMSO)

Seneca, Joseph J. and Michael J. Taussig (1971), 'Family Equivalence Scales and Personal Income Tax Exemptions for Children', 53 *Review of Economics and Statistics*, 253–62

Shelford's Treatise on the Law of Marriage, Divorce and Registration (1841)

Sorensen, A. and M. MacDonald (1982), 'Does Child Support Support the Children', 4 *Children and Youth Services Review*, 53

Spanier, Graham B. and Paul C. Glick (1981), 'Marital Instability in the United States: some correlations and recent changes', 30 *Family Relations*, 29

ten Broek, J. (1964), 'California's Dual System of Family Law: Its Origin, Development and Present Status', 16 *Stanford Law Rev.* 256–87

Thornes, Barbara and Jean Collard (1979), *Who Divorces?* (London, Routledge)

Todd, J.E. and L.M. Jones (1972), *Poverty in the United Kingdom* (Harmondsworth, Penguin Books)

Townsend, Peter (1979), *Poverty in the United Kingdom* (Harmondsworth, Penguin Books)

US Department of Health, Education and Welfare (1976), *Income Supplement Program: 1974 HEW Welfare Replacement Proposal*, Technical Analysis Paper 11 (Office of Income Security Policy, Washington DC)

van Slooten, R. and A.G. Coverdale (1978), 'The characteristics of low income households', *Social Trends* No.8 (London, HMSO)

Wadsworth, M.E.J. (1979), 'Early life events and later behavioural outcomes', in S.B. Sells *et al.* (eds.), *Human Functioning in Longitudinal Perspective* (Baltimore, Williams and Wilkins)

Wadsworth, M.E.J. (1984), 'Early stress and associations with adult behaviour and parenting', in W.R. Butler and B.D. Corver (eds.) *Stress and Disability in Childhood* (Bristol, John Wright and Sons)

Weale, Albert, Jonathan Bradshaw, Alan Maynard, and David Piachaud (1984), *Lone Mothers, Paid Work and Social Security* (London, Bedford Square Press)

Weitzman, Lenore, J. and Ruth Dixon (1980), 'The Alimony Myth: Does No-fault Divorce Make a Difference?', 14 *Family Law Quarterly*, 141

Weitzman, Lenore J. (1981), 'The Economics of Divorce: Social and Economic Consequences of Property, Alimony and Child Support Awards', 8 *UCLA Law Rev.*, 1181

Weitzman, Lenore J. (1984), 'Divorce Outcomes in the United States and England: A Comparative Analysis of Property and Maintenance Awards', in John M. Eekelaar and Sanford N. Katz (eds.), *The Resolution of Family Conflict: Comparative Legal Perspectives* (Toronto, Butterworths)

Weitzman, Lenore J. (1985), *The Divorce Revolution: The Unexpected Social and Economic Consequences for Women and Children in America* (New York, The Free Press/Macmillan)

Wynn, Margaret (1972), *Family Policy* (London, Michael Joseph)

Young, Edward M. (1983), 'Threshold Issues Associated with the Parental Obligation of Child Support', in Judith Cassetty (ed.), *The Parental Child Support Obligation* (Lexington, Lexington Books)

Zuckerman, A. (1978), 'Ownership of the Matrimonial Home: Common Sense or Reformist Nonsense', 94 *Law Quarterly Rev.* 26

Index